ANGELS DARK AND LIGHT

Angels Dark and Light

Gary Kinnaman

Servant Publications
Ann Arbor, Michigan

Unless otherwise noted, Scripture used in this work is taken from the *New International Version* of the Bible, (c) 1978 by New York International Bible Society, used by permission of Zondervan Bible publishers. Other versions quoted are as follows: *The King James Version*; *the Amplified Bible,* Zondervan Publishing; and *The New Testament in Modern English* by J.B. Phillips, Geoffrey Bles, Ltd.

Vine Books is an imprint of Servant Publications especially designed to serve evangelical Christians.

Published by Servant Publications
P.O. Box 8617
Ann Arbor, Michigan 48107

Cover design by Multnomah Graphics/Printing
Illustrations by Gustave Doré
Page layout by Diane Bareis

94 95 96 97 98 10 9 8 7 6 5 4 3 2 1

Printed in the United States of America
ISBN 0-89283-846-9

Library of Congress Cataloging-in-Publication Data

Kinnaman, Gary.
   Angels dark and light / Gary Kinnaman.
      p.   cm.
   "Vine books."
   Includes bibliographical references and index.
   ISBN 0-89283-846-9 :
   1. Angels.   2. Angels–Biblical teaching.   I. Title.
BT966.2.K56 1994
235'.3–dc20   94-25610
                                               CIP

Dedication

To my wife
Marilyn
and to her mother
Irene Rope
who went to be with the angels
July, 1991

Other Books by Gary Kinnaman

Overcoming the Dominion of Darkness
And Signs Shall Follow

Contents

Preface

My search for angels has taken me on quite a journey. I've been to the *lower* basement (that's below the upper basement) in the library at Fuller Theological Seminary in Pasadena. I've looked for older angels in books and magazines, and newer angels in computerized literature searches on CD-ROM. I've looked in public libraries and a huge university library. I have surveyed hundreds of people—Protestants and Catholics, charismatics and the not-so-charismatic. In my quest to find angels, I even visited a Benedictine monastery in a place in Oregon called, yes, *Mount Angel*.

And what did I find? I have yet to see an angel.

But I have read about many people who have seen them. And I've met a few, too. I've also discovered that there is a great deal more written about angels than I could have imagined, which made me wonder why I was writing another book. Gustav Davidson's *A Dictionary of Angels*, for example, includes a twenty-four page bibliography of angel books!

Some books and articles I read were skeptical. Some were downright scornful. Others, denying the "real" existence of cherubim or seraphim, viewed angels as metaphors of the presence of God. Still others were insightful, even theologically profound. Thomas Aquinas, who wrote his *Summa Theologica* in the thirteenth century, was nearly impossible for me to understand. One writer called the philosophical angelology of St. Thomas "the most brilliant piece of speculation on the subject produced by a Western theologian."

I also found, to my dismay, very few recently published *Christian* books on angels. This was especially disturbing when, in a very short visit to B. Dalton Bookseller and Waldenbooks in our local mall, I found five hot-selling books on angels, not one of them Christian. Oh yes, each of those two book stores had the nearly twenty-year-old book on angels by Billy Graham, of which two million copies have been sold.

So I have come full circle. In this book I explore a whole range of angel issues while maintaining a commitment to the Bible as our only gauge of truth. This is especially important when we talk about specific angelic encounters. I have collected a file full of angel stories, some of which have been startlingly wonderful, others terribly bizarre. I've included only those which fit into the scheme of biblical angelology. You might also like to know that I have included only first-hand stories. You know, there are a lot of angel stories out there that are four or five times told—and generously embellished. I have tried, in every example, to select only stories shared with me by the person or people who actually had the experience. I also tried to use stories from credible people, those who have not made a habit of seeing angels. Very few people have had actual experiences with angels, and those who have seen the lights of heaven have seen them only once, sometimes twice in a lifetime. Those kinds of stories were of the most interest to me.

I also would like to acknowledge the help of lots of people, without whom this book would not have been written. The support of my family is foremost in my mind. I have written several books, but it's quite amazing how quickly one forgets how time-consuming and overwhelming a project of this nature can be.

Thanks to our church board and staff for allowing me the time and freedom to do this work. Thanks to Rick Linamen, an associate pastor at Scottsdale Bible Church, for distributing my angel surveys in a couple of their adult classes. Thanks to

Doug and Susan Monet, wonderful Christian neighbors who helped me by circulating my angel survey in their circle of Catholic friends. Thanks to my secretary, Penny Jo Budd, for all the little things she did to help me during the last year. Thanks to Dr. Bill Yarger and the administration of Western Seminary, Phoenix, who allowed me to work this book into my Doctor of Ministry program; and to Dr. Kem Oberholtzer and Dr. Norm Wakefield, for their careful theological review of the manuscript. Thanks to Beth Feia and Heidi Hess at Servant Books for their excellent editorial assistance. And many, many thanks to all the people who told me about their angel experiences.

I only wish I could have included them all.

CHAPTER ONE

Frosted Glass: The Enigma of Reality

Angels belong to a uniquely different dimension of creation which we, limited to the natural order, can scarcely comprehend. **Billy Graham**

Was that an angel? What happened? Did *anything* happen?

Many spiritual experiences are elusive. Now you see them. Now you don't.

And sometimes they're not even spiritual.

A few years ago, after a Sunday evening service, an elderly woman wanted to talk to me. She looked distressed. "Bright, star-like objects," she reported as quietly as she could, "are floating across my bathroom window. Am I seeing a vision? Are they angels? Does this have some spiritual meaning?"

Her questions seemed a little odd to me. *She* seemed a little odd! But I'm always careful not to downplay another person's spiritual experiences. Knowing that the Bible itself is full of unusual stories of heaven's dimension intersecting earth, most of us are genuinely hoping for real encounters with God and his angels. Yet I had a sense, in the case of this dear lady, that this was not one of those encounters.

I asked her cautiously and politely, "Do you have frosted glass in your bathroom window?"

"Why, yes, I think I do," she replied timidly.

"Double check," I told her. "If you have frosted glass in your bathroom, what you're seeing could be the diffused lights of passing cars. I may be wrong, but I really don't think you are seeing anything unusual."

Spiritual experiences are mysterious. Often something that seems supernatural or paranormal can be easily explained. Or if something unusual occurs, the moment may be so transitory that we can't remember exactly what happened. But sometimes the reality of the spiritual realm bursts through the barrier of time and space.

The service was over. I had just opened my eyes after the closing prayer when I noticed a young mother hurrying up the aisle of the church. She could not hide her excitement. Her twelve-year-old son, she announced, had just seen two angels—*with me*—on the platform.

"Could I ask Matt a few questions?" I queried. Her son was still standing in the back of the church, looking a little embarrassed by his mother's enthusiasm.

I knew the family fairly well. This young man was level-headed, not overly religious.

"There were two of them," he reported without a jot of emotion.

"Were they standing or sitting? And where?" I wanted to know the specifics. Maybe he was just making this up.

"They were standing, one on either side of you."

I pressed him: "Were they large or small?"

"Large."

How large?

"*Very* large."

Larger than me?

"Oh, yes, *much* larger than you."

His straight face and quick, precise responses told me that this young man had really seen something. For a fleeting moment, God pulled back the curtain of time and space and let him see heavenly beings of light.

Much the same thing happened a few years later. I had just recounted this same story in one of my sermons. A member of our church, Tina Esman, wrote to me some time after the fact,

As soon as you finished telling the story of the little boy who saw angels with you on the platform, it was like my eyes were opened and I saw two big angels, two or three times larger than a human, in white robes with white hair, sitting on each side of you.

Then I believe the Lord revealed to me they were there to protect the very words of God that you would speak to his people. It was like the glory of the Lord or a golden haze was coming down from heaven between the angels and out through you to the people.

At first, I wanted to tell you about this, but I refrained. I thought that you would think I was weird, but as sure as I can still see it in my mind today, I know God is still protecting his words through you—even though I have never seen the same thing since.

Do angels exist? Absolutely. Do these incidents "prove" there are angels? No. Anymore than they prove, or even suggest, that I'm somebody special because others have seen angels stand with me when I preach. Unfortunately, or maybe fortunately, I've never seen them myself. Do stories like this, however, affirm what we know about spiritual reality from the Bible? Yes.

O world invisible, we view thee
O world intangible, we touch thee
O world unknowable, we know thee
Inapprehensible, we clutch thee!

Francis Thompson

Dietrich Bonhoeffer, one of the great Christian thinkers of this century, once wrote of miracles and providential events, "Believers see a sign. Unbelievers see nothing." The apostle Paul met Christ face to face, and yet the "men traveling with Saul stood there speechless; they heard the sound *but did not see anyone*" (Acts 9:7). One man, seeing the light, changed the course of history. Others just stood around blinking and bewildered.

What to one person is an authentic, life-changing event, is to another evidence of mental instability. As Paul was defending himself after his arrest—and recounting his remarkable conversion experience—Festus, the Roman governor of Judea, interrupted him with a shout, "You are out of your mind, Paul! Your great learning is driving you insane" (Acts 26:24).

Spiritual experiences are elusive. Paul said it this way, "For now we see through a glass, darkly; but then face to face" (1 Cor 13:12, KJV). Writing about angels is like looking through frosted glass: We know there's something on the other side, but we are not always sure what it is. Our humanity has limitations.

We can't look into the spiritual realm whenever we want, or see even one of its millions of spiritual beings at our whim. Nor can we see magnetic fields, or electricity, or the sun on a cloudy day. Reality is not based solely on what we can or cannot see, what we can or cannot understand.

Christian author Frederick Buechner writes,

> Sleight-of-hand magic is based on the demonstrable fact that as a rule people see only what they expect to see. Angels are powerful spirits whom God sends into the world to wish us well. Since we don't expect to see them, we don't. An angel spreads his glittering wings over us, and we say things like "It was one of those days that made you feel good just to be alive," or "I had a hunch everything was going to turn out all right," or "I don't know where I ever found the courage."[1]

The spiritual realm is so enigmatic that some people, even people who believe in God, have wondered if angels exist at all! Some theologians believe, for example, that angels are best understood as metaphors of God's presence, that there are really no angels in a perpetual state of heavenly existence. Instead, angels come and go like dreams, holographic wisps of the will of God. Created by God for a second or two, they carry messages and then vanish forever.

This is not, however, what we find in the Bible. The Bible consistently speaks of angels as real spiritual beings with individual existences, as we shall examine in detail throughout this book. Christian theologian C. Fred Dickason observes that never, even in the earliest writings of the Bible, "are angels considered mere illusions or figures of speech. They are an integral part of the story of God's dealing with men."[2]

Yet philosophical speculations about the existence and nature of angels abound. It's only natural, I suppose, because human beings are inquisitive to the core, especially about things that are mysterious and not fully explainable. A book on angels would not be complete without mentioning *The Celestial Hierarchy*, written by Dionysius, sometimes called St. Denis. A shadowy figure of early church history, Dionysius set out to examine and rank angels in great detail. Starting with the Bible, Dionysius added a good bit of medieval superstition about the spirit world. What resulted was an elaborate but fanciful hierarchy of spirit beings that essentially shaped the Christian view of angels for centuries.

Thomas Aquinas, known generally as "the father of Roman Catholic theology" and sometimes called "the Angel Doctor," was greatly influenced by the writings of Dionysius. He devoted a significant portion of his classic work *Summa Theologica* (which means, loosely, everything you ever wanted to know about theology) to scrutinizing and refining the views of Dionysius, including such things as "the predication, multiplication, and individuation of angel natures."

Some theologians were unimpressed with the findings of these men. Karl Barth called the writings of Dionysius "annoying," and in response to the complicated writings of Thomas Aquinas on angels Barth declared, "Holy Scripture gives us quite enough to think of regarding angels."[3]

In other words, there are some things about angels we can know with certainty, because of what is revealed in the Bible, but there are other things about which we can only speculate. Uncertain things about angels may be at best interesting and helpful, or at worst misleading. If we are going to understand angels dark and light, we need to know what is true and what is false, what is safe and what is dangerous. *What Christians believe about angels, or anything else for that matter, must be firmly grounded in the Bible.* Paul warned the Colossian church,

> Do not let anyone who delights in false humility and the worship of angels disqualify you for the prize. Such a person goes

into great detail about what he has seen, and his unspiritual mind puffs him up with idle notions.   **Colossians 2:18**

Paul is telling us here that, if we are not careful, truth as it is revealed in Scripture can be blurred by giving too much attention to "idle notions." So throughout this book, we will be examining everything about angels, and what different people say and believe about angels, in the light of Holy Scripture. Some things are clear. Many things are not.

God created the angels to serve him and his people. If there is anything we can learn from the Bible about angels, it's that they are *real*. Angels exist. And yet there are theologians who have wondered about this (although you probably know that theologians wonder about a lot of things). Because angels come and go like a smudge of smoke on a windy day, some have speculated that angels do not actually have a "nature," or an independent existence. Some theologians believe that angels exist momentarily, just to deliver a message. Or, to say it another way, the angel *is* the message. Once the message is given, the angel vanishes forever, or until God "recreates" him to send another message. Angels, according to this view, don't really "exist."

One writer has noted, "It has often been pointed out that angels do not have biographies. They do not have horizontal, historical narrative extension. They are not... developmental. They break into time, breaking time and plot, and then, as the story in Luke says, disappear without a trace, leaving only a song/image."[4] I find this idea hard to accept, because the Bible teaches that angels exist in the presence of God, even when they are not busy bringing messages to earth.

The great reformer John Calvin sternly repudiated "that nugatory [trifling!] philosophy concerning the holy angels which teaches that they are nothing but inspirations or good motivations by God in the minds of men."[5]

Yet the Bible is silent on "the 'nature' of angels, whether or not they are persons, or what their relationship is to the physical world."[6] All we know is that they are invisible spiritual beings who minister to God and his people.

Discounting the idea of marriage in heaven, Jesus came the closest to talking about "the nature" of angels when he explained, "But those who are considered worthy of taking part in that age [to come] and in the resurrection from the dead will neither marry nor be given in marriage, and they can no longer die; *for they are like the angels*."[7] This tells us only that angel "nature" is immortal, nothing else. And it implies that angels have a separate, ongoing existence.

Angels, then, are real. Angels are spiritual beings, godlike but not God. Nor are they human, or fleshy, although they may appear in human form. The precise "substance" of their nature is unknown. They are immortal. They are not *omnipresent*—everywhere present at the same time, like God, but they are *immediately* present. In Matthew 4:11 we are told that angels "came" to minister to Jesus after his temptations in the wilderness, suggesting that the angels were not present when the devil had appeared just minutes before. God was there, in the incarnate Son—but angels were not. Angels are not everywhere.

IF HEAVEN IS SO CLOSE, WHY DOES GOD SEEM SO FAR AWAY?

We see heaven through frosted glass. This is, perhaps, the most terrible and frustrating consequence of human sin. When God first created Adam and Eve, immediate fellowship and direct conversation with heaven was "normal." There were no barriers. But the Serpent, "more crafty than any of the wild animals the Lord God had made," challenged the woman—and God: "You will not surely die (if you eat of the tree of the knowledge of good and evil). For God knows that when you eat of it your eyes will be opened, and you will be like God, knowing good and evil (italics mine)."[8]

Your eyes will be opened. What eyes? What will they see? It seems like the devil is making her an offer to become more *spiritually* perceptive, more like God. Ironically, Adam and Eve did not get what they saw, didn't see what they were going to get. That's always the nature of illusion—the bait of truth always hides the hook of deception. Just like the devil predicted, "the eyes of both of them were opened."

But they did not become more godlike. Instead, for the first time, "they realized they were naked." The focus of human perception reverted from the primacy of the spiritual dimension to the time and space limitations of the physical creation. The material world clicked on. The spiritual dimension faded into a blind haze. Essentially, human nature was turned upside down.

We see heaven—and angels—through frosted glass. Former *New York Times* reporter, McCandlish Phillips, observed that we can only know what God elects to reveal to us "about the spiritual and supernatural.... We can know nothing about angels... apart from revelation."[9] "Rumors of angels" is how one author recently described the shadowy beings of the spiritual realm.[10]

It's like our spiritual eyes need cataract surgery, and the milky film keeps thickening. For the past couple of generations our western culture has scorned spiritual experiences. For those of us raised under the influence of scientific materialism, the frosted glass is tinted black. Every mystery is vaporized in the acid vat of scientific inquiry. Though North Americans believe in God in theory, the spiritual realm is not practically real to us. Even our language, a vital component of our culture, betrays our skepticism about "spiritual things." The terms "supernatural" and "paranormal" are, in fact, western creations. These expressions suggest that we have created an artificial distinction between "natural" and "supernatural," "normal" and "paranormal."

It may come as a surprise that the English word "supernatural" has no equivalent in either the Hebrew of the Old Testament or the Greek of the New Testament. For the writers of the Bible, even though they, too, looked through dark glass, the boundary between time and eternity was not nearly so sharply defined. Nor is it so clearly defined in nonwestern cultures. In India, for example, there is no word for "paranormal" or "supernatural" in any of its fourteen major languages.[11]

The blurry boundary between time and eternity was the underlying theme in the hugely successful film, *Field of Dreams*. In this movie, a resonant god-like voice guides star Kevin Costner to build a baseball diamond in the middle of an Iowa cornfield. Great ball players, all deceased, begin materializing out of the tall rows of late-season corn on the edge of the playing field.

One of the players, literally a ghost from the past, asks Kevin Costner incredulously, "Is this heaven?"

Costner's response will be immortalized: "No," he says, just as incredulously, "*This is Iowa!*"

The boundary between heaven and earth had vanished. The movie, of course, is not Christian. It is New Age to the core,* but New Agers are trying to tell us that we can rediscover, if we try, the reality of the spiritual dimension. It's just beyond the next row of corn.

This is, in fact, very close to the biblical worldview—not that we can converse with the dead, but that "the kingdom of God is *at hand.*" Heaven is as near as our breath. Angels are as close as the other side of the room—or, sometimes, closer still.

FOUR KINDS OF CLOSE ENCOUNTERS

The faint image of heaven is on the other side of the dark

---

*"New Age" is a term which has been used to apply broadly to a number of interrelated, non-Christian religious and quasi-religious beliefs which are becoming increasingly popular.[12]

glass. We know something is there! What do we see? And how do we see it? I've come to believe, to borrow from UFO terminology, that there are four kinds of supernatural "close encounters."

First, God sometimes puts thoughts in our heads. This most common kind of spiritual encounter is not overtly supernatural, but the Bible contains many examples. In one instance, when Jesus was alone with his disciples, he asked them what people were saying about him. "Some say you are John the Baptist," they replied. "Others say Elijah; and still others, Jeremiah or one of the prophets."

"But what about you?" he asked. "Who do you say I am?"

Peter had a thought. "You are the Christ, the Son of the living God," he blurted.

"This was not revealed to you by man, but by my Father in heaven," (Mt 16:13-17) Jesus explained, making it quite clear that Peter's thought was not, in fact, Peter's thought. It came from the heavenlies. The Father in heaven had placed the thought in Peter's mind.

Now, God does not control our thoughts, but he does speak to us from time to time. And while this kind of spiritual illumination doesn't make a lot of headlines—it's not very sensational—we could call this *a supernatural encounter of the first kind.*

Second, heaven may come to us in mental images and dreams. We "see" pictures inside our heads, on a kind of mental television screen. Dreams, of course, have always been a matter of fascination and study, from the oldest accounts in the Bible to contemporary scientific research. Some say they are purely physiological, chemically induced impressions. Others contend that sometimes dreams are windows to heaven, a clear teaching of the Bible. While most dreams are a normal function of a sleeping brain, and most dreams are without spiritual significance, in the Bible God uses dreams from time to time to speak to people. References to dreams occur over one hundred times in Scripture, and angels are occasionally in those dreams.[13]

Jacob had a famous angel dream. Fleeing his vengeful brother Esau, Jacob left Beersheba and set out for Haran. "When he reached a certain place, he stopped for the night because the sun had set. Taking one of the stones there, he put it under his head and lay down to sleep. *He had a dream* in which he saw a stairway resting on the earth, with its top reaching to heaven, *and the angels of God were ascending and descending*" (Gn 28:11-12, italics mine).

Joseph, after the visit of the Magi, was warned in a dream by an angel, "Get up, take the child [Jesus] and his mother and escape to Egypt. Stay there until I tell you, for Herod is going to search for the child to kill him" (Mt 2:13).

When a friend of mine, Mark Buckley, heard I was writing about angels, he asked me reluctantly if I might be interested in a story about how an angel appeared to him in a dream. "Hundreds of people were impacted by my dream," he told me. Mark is a successful—and level-headed—pastor in the Phoenix area and a regular feature writer for *Ministries Today* magazine.

In the spring of 1971 I lived in Novato, California, with five other men in a Christian ministry house called Solid Rock. One night I had a dream that changed the course of my life and ministry. In my dream I saw a group of students playing volleyball in the Terra Linda High School gym. I had graduated from Terra Linda High three years before, so I remembered the gym well.

While I was observing the ebb and flow of the game, a handsome man's face suddenly appeared in my dream. "Be here tomorrow night at 7:30," he said. Then the face disappeared and the dream ended.

When I woke up the next morning, I remembered the

dream vividly. I felt like the Lord had spoken to me. Since the face I had seen did not look like Jesus, I thought it might have been an angel. When my good friend Malcolm woke up, I told him about my dream and asked him if he would accompany me to Terra Linda High that night. Malcolm was not at all sure that I had heard from the Lord, but he was willing to come along and support me.

Malcolm and I arrived at the high school at 7:15 that evening. The campus was deserted, except for a few drama students setting up for a play. We tried the door of the gym. Locked. Carrying some gospel tracts, we walked aimlessly around the school buildings. I didn't know what the Lord had in store for me, but I assumed I was supposed to share the gospel with someone.

At 7:30 we went and stood on the curb in front of the gym. I was feeling pretty dumb. Malcolm was rubbing it in. Laughingly, he chided, "I guess you missed it this time."

Just as we were about to leave, a school bus pulled over to the curb in front of us. One by one the members of the Terra Linda High baseball team got off the bus. We walked over and began giving our tracts to the young men, who weren't very receptive to the gospel. They were returning from a long game and eager to get their showers. Only a couple of them stopped long enough to listen as we attempted to share the gospel.

Don Lucas, the coach, was the last man off the bus. Don, who had been my coach for two years when I played varsity football and baseball, broke into a big smile when he recognized me. Our joy in seeing one another was multiplied when he told me that he, too, had recently given his life to Christ. After mentioning he was forming a Fellowship of Christian Athletes at his school, he rushed off to join the players in the locker room.

When the driver pulled the empty school bus away from

the curb, Malcolm and I decided to leave too. I had this empty feeling inside me. It was great to see my old coach, but nothing dramatic had happened. I just assumed I had misinterpreted my dream.

Two weeks later I got a call from Don. "How would you like to speak at our Christian Athletes meeting?" he asked. I accepted enthusiastically. At that meeting, a week later, I met another Christian coach, who was also a health education teacher at the high school. Hearing that I had been hospitalized a few years before, after a drug overdose, he invited me to speak to his classes about the dangers of drug abuse and what Jesus did to deliver me from drug addiction.

The day I spoke at the school, I met several other teachers who also asked me to visit their classes. One open door kept leading to another. Some days I would speak to as many as five different classes of students!

I was given unusual freedom to share my faith—along with an anti-drug message—at the school. Within a few months, the students formed a lunch-time Bible study in one of the classrooms. They asked me to come once a week and teach them. I was with them every week for the next two years!

Recommendations from the teachers at Terra Linda High opened the door for me to speak to health education, history, and science classes at San Rafael, Redwood, Drake, and Tamalpias High Schools. Soon we had weekly Bible studies going at four different schools. Marin County, just north of San Francisco, has always had a liberal climate, but in the early 1970s the teachers and principals of the high schools in Marin welcomed the gospel as a means to help the students.

I am still in contact with many of the students who trusted Christ for eternal life and were discipled through those high school Bible studies. Some have entered full time Christian ministry. When I think back to how it all began, I can still picture in my mind the face of the angel who directed me to "be here tomorrow at 7:30."

Mark had a *supernatural encounter of the second kind.*

Third, heaven may come to us in visions and trances. These are less common and more extraordinary than dreams and mental images. I think of a vision as something external, something visual we "see" *outside* us, as opposed to dreams and images *inside* our heads. The Bible does not make this distinction in every case, but we have the sense from some passages that what people saw was like "virtual reality." It wasn't really there, but it was real enough, perhaps three-dimensional and in full color. A vision or trance is a *supernatural encounter of the third kind.*

The apostle Peter, visiting friends in Joppa on the Mediterranean coast, went up on the roof of the house to catch a little sea breeze and pray. "He became hungry and wanted something to eat, and while the meal was being prepared, he fell into a trance." For whatever reason, the Bible text says nothing about Peter falling asleep or dreaming. It uses the unique term "trance." The Greek term is *ekstasis*, from which we derive the English word "ecstasy."

Beyond himself, Peter "saw heaven opened and something like a large sheet being let down to earth by its four corners. It contained all kinds of four-footed animals, as well as reptiles of the earth and birds of the air." Nonkosher junk food, like hot dogs and bacon. "Then a voice told him, 'Get up, Peter. Kill and eat.'.... This happened three times, and immediately the sheet was taken back to heaven" (Acts 10:9-16). The sheet, apparently, was not in Peter's mind. It came from heaven and went back to heaven.

Now the account, of course, is about how God wanted Peter to share the gospel with the "unclean" Gentiles, something a good

Jew like Peter was not about to do. But the point I'm making is that what appeared here was a kind of three-dimensional image.

Perhaps John had a similar experience when, "in the Spirit" on the Lord's Day, he wrote the book of Revelation. When I read the last book of the Bible, it gives me the impression that John saw and heard things *outside* his own mind, trancelike.

Much of what he saw must have been similar to "virtual reality": the Antichrist rising from the sea, or a beast with "ten horns and seven heads, with ten crowns on his horns" (Rv 13:1). But other things John saw were, I believe, really there: "Then I looked and heard the voice of many angels, numbering thousands upon thousands, and ten times ten thousand. They encircled the throne... In a loud voice they sang: 'Worthy is the Lamb who was slain'" (Rv 5:11-12). John really saw that. It was really there.

Fourth, on the highest level of spiritual encounter, heaven's reality literally may breach time and space. Jesus appeared, literally, to Saul (later named the apostle Paul) on the road to Damascus. My uncle became a Christian when Jesus appeared, literally, standing at the foot of his bed. Like Paul, my uncle did not wait a month or two to think about what had happened. His vision of Christ was compelling, and he became a Christian that night. This was a *supernatural encounter of the fourth kind*, typical of most of the angel appearances in the Bible.

Angels appeared, literally, to many people in the Bible. They could be seen and heard, and people talked with them like you would talk with a friend. As I have collected reports of angel encounters and surveyed hundreds of people, I have discovered that very few individuals have had an unmistakably real and literal encounter with an angel. And most of those who have, have seen an angel only once. Real spiritual encounters of the fourth kind are rare.

Moreover, when they do occur, it may be difficult, even

impossible, for the individual to describe the experience. For example, the apostle Paul apparently had an out-of-the-body experience, probably when he was stoned at Lystra (Acts 14:19-20). He recounts, "I know a man [Paul is referring to himself] in Christ who fourteen years ago was caught up to... heaven. Whether in the body or apart from the body I do not know.... He heard *inexpressible things, things that man is not permitted to tell*" (italics mine).[14]

It is not merely God who is incomprehensible; the same can also be said of heaven within the creaturely world.

Karl Barth

Human language simply cannot describe that which is beyond normal human experience. Relying on the language of simile and metaphor, Ezekiel described his Majesty's private chambers:

I looked, and I saw a windstorm coming out of the north—an immense cloud with flashing lightning and surrounded by brilliant light. The center of the fire looked *like* glowing metal, and in the fire was what looked *like* four living creatures. *In appearance* their *form* was that of a man, but each of them had four faces and four wings. Their legs were straight; their feet were *like* those of a calf and gleamed *like* burnished bronze.... Then there came a voice from above the expanse over their heads as they stood with lowered wings. Above the expanse over their heads was what looked *like* a throne of sapphire, and high above on the throne was a figure *like* that of a man. I saw that from what *appeared* to be his waist up he looked *like* glowing metal, *as if* full of fire, and that from there down he looked *like* fire; and brilliant light surrounded him. *Like* the appearance of a rainbow in the clouds on a rainy day, so was the radiance around him. This was *the appearance* of *the likeness* of glory of the Lord.

Ezekiel 1:4-7, 25-28 (italics mine)

Notice especially the last line. Ezekiel didn't see the Lord. He didn't even see the glory of the Lord. In fact, he didn't even see the likeness of the glory of the Lord. Ezekiel beheld *the appearance of the likeness of the glory of the Lord!* This is another example of the highest form of spiritual experience. Heaven broke into time and space, and Ezekiel saw the throne of God—literally. It was like a toddler trying to describe a dazzling ride at Disneyland. Ezekiel had no previous experience or a point of reference to describe what he had seen.

In another Old Testament narrative (2 Kings 6:8-23), the king of Aram, frustrated and enraged by Elisha's prophetic guidance of the king of Israel, set out to abduct his Jewish nemesis. "Go, find out where [Elijah] is," the king ordered, "so I can send men and capture him." The report came back: "He is in Dothan." So the king of Aram sent a strong force of horsemen and chariots and surrounded the city in the middle of the night. The next morning, when Elisha's understudy awoke to find the city of Dothan under siege, he was terrified. "Oh, my lord, what shall we do?" he quivered.

"Don't be afraid," the prophet answered with confidence. "Those who are with us are more than those who are with them." And Elisha prayed, "O Lord, *open his eyes so he may see.*" God did just that, and the young man saw—literally—into the spiritual dimension: the hills around the city were full of heavenly horses and chariots of fire sent to protect Elisha. It wasn't a dream. It wasn't imagery. The fiery hosts of the Lord were really there.

So God may reveal himself to us in different ways and on different levels, from subliminal thoughts to literal angelic appearances. George Washington may have had a supernatural encounter of the fourth kind. He was said to have had an angel appear to him at Valley Forge. Johnny Cash has told of being visited by angels—twice, once when he was twelve and again as an adult. Each time the angel warned him of an impending death. And then there's the story (I couldn't get a first hand report on this one) of six Russian cosmonauts—all atheists—who, while in space, twice sighted a band of angels with wings as big as jumbo jets![15]

People still hear the voice of God and see angels. Theologian C. Fred Dickason writes, "The combined witness of the Scriptures, the Old and New Testaments, and of the Savior, assures us that there is a world of intelligent, powerful, invisible creatures about us and above us that warrants our prayerful and careful study and challenges us to expand our categories of thought and to change our conduct of life in accord with God's truth."[16]

CHAPTER TWO

God's Last Word on Angels

The doctrinal sphere [angels and spirit beings] which we have to enter and traverse in this section is the most remarkable and difficult of all.... Holy Scripture gives us quite enough to think of regarding angels. **Karl Barth**

Our frame of reference must be the scriptures as our supreme authority on this subject.
Billy Graham

We're not really sure when or even why God created angels. Angels are not mentioned anywhere in the six days of creation in Genesis 1, unless they are somehow implied by "the lights in the expanse of the sky" (Gn 1:14-19). In Job, for example, the parallelism of the ancient Hebrew poetry makes angels and stars almost synonymous:

> Where were you when I laid the earth's foundation?
>> Tell me, if you understand.
> Who marked off its dimensions?
>> Surely you know!
> Who stretched a measuring line across it?
>> On what were its footings set,
>> or who laid its cornerstone—
> *while the morning stars sang together*
> *and all the angels shouted for joy?*[1]

Actually, angels are not stars, and stars are not angels, but they are closely associated with one another in the older portions of the Bible,[2] which may suggest that God created angels—with the stars—on the fourth day of Creation.

It is also possible that God created the angels *before* the creation of the heavens and the earth in Genesis 1. The Bible does not tell us this outright, but perhaps it is assumed by the appearance of Satan in the Garden of Eden. Who is this evil being and how did he get there? When did he fall out of God's favor? What is evil power doing in God's new and sinless earth? Some scholars believe that some of the angels, created long before Genesis 1, fell out of God's favor and later landed on the earth. Other Christian theologians think that the fall of the angels may have taken place sometime between Genesis 2 and 3, between the creation of man and the encounter with the Serpent in the Garden of Eden.

In any case, it seems that a war in the heavenlies between good and evil angels was already well established before God created Adam. The creation mandate, for example, *to have dominion over all the earth*, could suggest spiritual warfare (Gn 1:26). Ruling over the earth had to mean more than caretaking and zookeeping. This becomes sinfully clear in Genesis 3, where the Serpent, more than just another animal, challenges the authority of God in the new earth.

So here is my suggested sequence of early history: (1) God created the angels and other heavenly beings. But we don't know exactly when. Paul wrote in Colossians 1:16, "For by him all things were created: things in heaven and on earth, visible and invisible.... all things were created by him and for him." (2) Some time later (we still don't know when), Satan, who may have started his career as an archangel, led a celestial rebellion against God. He lost. (3) Lastly, God created the material heavens and the earth and everything in them, including humans. Somewhere along they way (we don't know when this happened either), the devil was hurled to the earth. All this is generally accepted by the church, even though much of the detail is not as clear in the Bible as we would like it to be.

Revelation 12:7-9 tells us,

And there was war in heaven. Michael and his angels fought against the dragon, and the dragon and his angels fought back. But he was not strong enough, and they lost their place in heaven. The great dragon was hurled down—that ancient serpent called the devil, or Satan, who leads the whole world astray. He was hurled to the earth, and his angels with him.

That this happened is clear. *When* it happened is not. We cannot be sure if this passage is describing a past or future event. While some believe this is a flashback to the fall of Satan before Creation, others feel this passage describes something that will take place sometime shortly before the end of the world, suggesting that Satan's power will be unleashed on the earth in unprecedented fury just before the return of Christ (see Rv 9:1-6).

Many Bible students think that Isaiah 14:12-15 may be a parallel:

How you have fallen from heaven,
    O morning star, son of the dawn!
You have been cast down to the earth,

You who once laid low the nations!
You said in your heart,
   "I will ascend to heaven;
I will raise my throne
   above the stars [the angels?] of God;
I will sit enthroned on the mount of the assembly
   [a reference to the Jewish temple mount, Zion],
   on the utmost heights of the sacred mountain.
I will ascend above the tops of the clouds;
   I will make myself like the Most High."
But you are brought down to the grave [Hebrew: *sheol,*
   or *hades,* the place of the dead]
   to the depths of the pit.

In its historical context, the passage you just read is a prophetic judgment against the king of Babylon. Yet it is often
understood to have a broader application to the prideful fall of
Satan. In the King James Version of the Bible, the phrase
"morning star" is translated "Lucifer."[3] Maybe Jesus was allud-
ing to this Old Testament text when he said to his disciples, "I
saw Satan fall like lightning from heaven. I have given you
authority to trample on snakes and scorpions and to overcome
all the power of the enemy" (Lk 10:18-19).

And Revelation 9:1-2 uses similar imagery. "The fifth angel
[of judgment] sounded his trumpet, and I saw a star[4] that had
fallen from the sky to the earth. The star [Satan] was given the
key to the shaft of the Abyss [another word for "the pit," or
"hades"]. When he opened the Abyss, smoke rose from it like
the smoke from a gigantic furnace."

So the Bible does not tell us, specifically and directly, when
God created the angels, or when the evil angels fell out of
heaven. But this we know: God is the Creator of all things,
including the angels, and somewhere along the line, many of
those angels turned evil.

Origen, one of the best known "fathers" of the very early
Church, didn't hide his perplexity about some of these ques-

tions: "This also is part of the teaching of the Church, that there are certain angels of God, and certain good influences, which are his servants in accomplishing the salvation of men. When these [angels], however, were created, or what nature they are, or how they exist, is not clearly revealed."[5]

The first *good* angels appear in Genesis 3. After God banished man from the Garden of Eden, "he placed on the east side of the Garden of Eden cherubim [several special angels[6]] and a flaming sword flashing back and forth to guard the way to the tree of life" (Gn 3:24). Billy Graham sums up the role of the good angels:

Have you ever seen or met one of these superior beings called angels? They are God's messengers whose chief business is to carry out his orders in the world. He has given them an ambassadorial charge. He has designed and empowered them as holy deputies to perform works of righteousness. In this way they assist him as their Creator while he sovereignly controls the universe. So he has given them the capacity to bring his holy enterprises into a successful conclusion.[7]

ANGEL TERMS USED IN THE BIBLE

Perhaps the best way to understand angels is to take a look at some of the different words for "angel" in the Hebrew and Greek testaments of the Bible. The English word "angel" is derived from *angelos*, a Greek term used nearly two hundred times in the New Testament and which means, very simply, "messenger."

In the Hellenistic world just prior to New Testament history, the term had little religious meaning, and the role of the human *angelos* was fairly simple: he delivered messages, answered questions, and expected payment for his services—and he was protected by the gods. The ancient human *angelos* could also be an envoy, making treaties and delivering official communiqués. In early Greek, philosophers—and sometimes even birds—were referred to as *angeloi!*[8]

The main idea in the New Testament is that *angeloi* (the plural form of *angelos*) are *divine* celestial beings with a message from God. Generally, this concept in the New Testament is taken from the Jewish ideas about angels in the Old Testament, that "angels are representatives of the heavenly world and are God's messengers. When they appear, the supernatural world breaks into this one."[9]

In the Old Testament, *malak* is the term used most frequently of angels. Like *angelos*, it means messenger, or representative. *Malaka* is the Hebrew word for work or business, and *malukut* means message (see Hg 1:13). Malachi, one of the Old Testament prophets, is a name that means "my messenger."

"Messenger" is the translation (but not the meaning) of *malak*. For us, the word "messenger" has little significance compared with the importance of the word in the ancient world. Because communication was so difficult—sometimes it took weeks to deliver a message (they didn't have phones or FAX machines!)—the messenger would often have to speak and even mediate for the one who sent him.

This is illustrated in Genesis 44. Joseph, one of the twelve sons of Jacob, had been sold into slavery by his brothers. Remarkably, Joseph wound up as prince of Egypt. When a terrible famine threatened the entire region, Joseph's estranged brothers ventured into Egypt looking for food, only to discover that their little brother had become a prominent government official. At first the brothers didn't recognize Joseph, although he recognized them. Speaking fluent Egyptian, Joseph kept himself disguised, and for reasons never fully explained in Scripture, he treated his brothers pretty roughly. (When you read the account, though, you really feel like they had it coming!)

Shortly before disclosing his real identity, Joseph sent his brothers on their way back home, their pack animals loaded with food. But in a ploy to arrest them, Joseph hid his golden chalice in their travel bags. When the servant discovered the "stolen" cup, one of the brothers, Judah, negotiated desperately with the servant—"the messenger" who represented Joseph. Actually, Judah was begging for Benjamin's life! It's as if the servant-messenger and his master, Joseph, were one.

In Genesis 24, Abraham sends his servant-messenger to another country to find a wife for his son Isaac. Can you imagine your father sending his secretary on a trip to California or New York, to find you a spouse?

The word "messenger" had so much more meaning in ancient culture than it does in ours. In the non-Christian Greek world, for example, "So much depended on the messenger, he was regarded as being under the special protection of the gods, which not only meant that to do harm to him was an act against the gods, but also meant that the messenger saw his task as a divine one....Little of this is conveyed by our word 'messenger.'"[10]

If someone were to ask me if I had ever seen an angel, I am afraid I could not give a very satisfying answer. But should I be asked if I ever met a messenger of God, then the answer would be an emphatic and unequivocal, "Yes, I have!"

Claus Westermann

So, in their simplest activity, angels are messengers. St. Augustine wrote,

> The Angels are spirits, but it is not because they are spirits that they are Angels. They become Angels when they are sent, for the name Angel refers to their office not to their nature. You ask the name of this nature, it is *spirit*; you ask its office, it is that of an Angel (i.e., messenger). In as far as he exists, an Angel is a spirit; in as far as he acts, he is an Angel.[11]

Forrester Church says it this way: "Remember, angels are

both God's messengers and God's message, witnesses to eternity in time, to the presence of the divine amidst the ordinary. Every moment of every day is riddled by their traces."[12]

Angels are in constant service to God. They may appear, literally, bringing a message of encouragement or guidance. Or they may come in disguise—"angels unawares," as the King James Bible puts it. Or, maybe you just had a really good day, and you're not sure why!

HOW MANY ANGELS ARE THERE?

We can only guess how many angels there may be. Some people have tried to guess exactly. Fourteenth-century mystics arrived at a precise figure—301,655,722—by employing elaborate but obscure calculations. Wild speculation like this governed theological studies during the middle centuries. Some of the early Lutherans, in a work called *Theatrium Diabolorum*,[13] estimated that there were 2.5 billion devils, a number later raised to 10,000 billion![14]

Millions of spiritual creatures walk the earth unseen,
both when we wake and when we sleep.
Milton, *Paradise Lost*, IV

The Bible, like everything else it says about angels, discloses the numbers of heavenly beings only in generalities. When Jesus was about to be arrested, he announced that, if he wanted to, he could call twelve legions of angels to his aid (Mt 26:53). In the time of Augustus Caesar, a legion numbered some six thousand men, so Jesus was talking about tens of thousands of angelic beings!

In Deuteronomy 33:2, Moses sings,

The Lord came from Sinai
  and dawned over them from Seir;
  he shown forth from Mount Paran.
He came with myriads of holy ones...

Jude 14 gives us a glimpse of the throngs of angels accompanying the advent of the Lord: "See, the Lord is coming with thousands upon thousands of his holy ones."

And in the last book of the Bible, John looked and heard "... the voice of many angels, numbering thousands upon thousands, and ten thousand times ten thousand" (Rv 5:11).

ANGELIC ORGANIZATION

Angels are described in hosts, but they are not without a system. Again, although the Bible is virtually silent on the arrangement of heaven, this has not discouraged speculative theologians—maybe we could call them "angelogians"—who have ranked the heavenly beings in elaborate schemes.

In *The Celestial Hierarchy*, Dionysius, writing in the sixth century, spun the speculative fabric of angelic orders in extraordinary detail, a heavenly table of organization that came to be viewed with great authority.

Catholics can trace their angelology back through Thomas Aquinas, whose ideas about angels were greatly influenced by Dionysius. Mortimer Adler, the general editor of the *Encyclopedia Britannica* and author of dozens of books, summarizes and simplifies Dionysius' scheme:

> The society or community of angels was divided into three hierarchies, and in each hierarchy there were three choirs or orders of angels; in the first and topmost hierarchy, seraphim, cherubim, and thrones, in descending order; in the second and middle hierarchy, dominions, virtues, and powers; in the third and bottom hierarchy, principalities, archangels, and angels.

Expressed in the simplest terms, the descending order of the hierarchies, and of the three choirs in each hierarchy, consisted in grades of creaturely perfection—the seraphim representing the highest grade of perfection among God's creatures, and mere angels the lowest. The perfection referred to was not moral, but metaphysical—a perfection in mode of being.[15]

Billy Graham's books are consistently biblical and reliable. Basing his ideas on Colossians 1:16 and other portions of the Bible, he suggests the following angelic organization: archangels, angels, seraphim, cherubim, principalities, authorities, powers, thrones, might, and dominion.[16] In the Colossians passage Paul writes, "For by him [Christ] all things were created, things in heaven and on earth, visible and invisible, whether thrones or powers or rulers or authorities."

This verse refers primarily to the authority of Christ over the kingdoms of this world; beyond that, it may refer to the principalities and powers of darkness which influence those kingdoms. Paul states in another of his letters, "For our struggle is not against flesh and blood, but against the rulers, against the authorities, against the powers of this dark world, and against the spiritual forces of evil in the heavenly realms" (Eph 6:12).

These Scriptures tell us that there are indeed heavenly hierarchies, but they are unclear about whether these are the heavenly offices of light or dark angels. It is impossible to determine these orders with certainty, as several Bible verses use different terms for the angelic hosts in different arrangements.

Theologian C. Fred Dickason notes that there "is enough evidence to say that there are distinct and graded ranks, but not enough evidence to make a complete comparison or organizational chart."[17] Speaking of the ranking and social order of angels, St. Augustine conceded, "Let those who are able answer these questions, if they can also prove their answers to be true; but as for me, I confess my ignorance."[18]

We do know with certainty a couple of things about angel

ranks: first, according to the first and second chapters of Hebrews, angels are much lower than God the Father and his Son, Jesus; and second, according to Psalm 8:5, human beings are "a little lower than the angels."[19]

MY LAST WORD ON GOD'S LAST WORD ON ANGELS

In summary, God created the angels, countless thousands of them, some time before he created the physical universe. In those mists of pre-time, a war in heaven resulted in the expulsion of Satan and his angels. Human beings were created in God's image, a little lower than the angels. Generally messengers of the word of the Lord, the good angels serve God and his people, while the evil angels plainly serve Satan and his purposes. And angels in both kingdoms—light and dark—are governed by rank and order.

But what do angels look like? In the next two chapters, we're going to paint a portrait of angels—and take a closer look at what they do for a living.

Angels Face to Face

The angels of God are bright and shining beings, emanating light and mirroring the glory of God.

Basilea Schlink

Real angels are not dull. They don't wear halos and strum harps and sing the same old song over and over again forever.

Forrester Church

A close friend—sensible and intelligent—handed me this angel report, on the condition that I not mention her name. It's an exceptional angel appearance that gives us an idea about what angels look like and what they do.

I heard you were looking for angel experiences. I hesitated to write to you, but decided to chance it. You may share my account if you desire, but only if you do so anonymously. I learned very quickly not to share it freely because of the adverse reactions I received.

About eight years ago, I was praying with another woman from my church. She had been tormented by feelings of inadequacy and inferiority for years. She had great doubts about God's love for her and forgiveness of her. She had received extensive Bible training and counsel, but seemed unable to break out of the depression caused by these doubts. Two of us went to pray for her at her home. We had fasted earlier in the week, but had eaten the previous day and that morning; I wanted us to be physically ready. In other words, what I am about to share with you was not a hallucination because of a lack of food!

We started the ministry session with worship. Then we prayed. We would pray, talk, pray, talk. The time went very quickly, although we were with our friend for several hours. We kept feeling that we had not gotten to the root, so we would pray again. Then my prayer partner had the sense that something had happened to our friend when she was being born. My recollection of what was said, exactly, is unclear, because my attention was being drawn away.

The presence of the Lord was really strong in the room. I had my eyes closed, but I realized I could see a glowing. It was like I could "see" a radiant being in front of me, right behind my prayer partner. I could also "feel" a heavenly presence behind me. I knew it was an angel, and I was awed.

I did nothing for a few minutes, waiting for the presence to go away. Then I opened my eyes, and I actually saw the being with my eyes open. He was very tall and shining and sort of transparent. He had on a robe of some kind. He had no hair on his face, and I think his hair was long and pulled back. I am sure this creature was an angel. I call him "he," and yet I knew it wasn't male.

I was a little scared and very awestruck. The angel seemed as tall as the ceiling. Then I turned slowly around, and there was another angel! This was the presence I had felt behind me. He was also very tall, seemed muscular in build, and had red hair, or hair like red. He was similarly dressed, except he had a huge drawn sword.

I was not exactly afraid, but overwhelmed, astonished, and intimidated completely. Then peace came over me, and I knew that these angels were there to protect and minister to us. I did not hear any voice, and the angels did not acknowledge me at all.

At this point my attention was drawn back to my prayer partner and the woman for whom we were praying, who was lying on the floor. My friend, praying for her as if she were having a baby, blurted out, "It's time for the birth!"

I know this sounds strange—this is why I have been so reluctant to share this story—but the woman, when we asked her what "the baby" looked like, began weeping and laughing. She said, "It's me, and I am beautiful and new." Then she said she knew she had been reborn.[1]

At this point I noticed that the angel behind my prayer partner had a brown bag. I was perplexed. Then my friend got a puzzled look, too, as she declared, "There's something more that God wants to do. The afterbirth has to come." The angel stepped forward, took what I "saw" as a brown-like mass, placed it in his bag, and left through the ceiling. The angel behind me followed him.

All during this experience, I said nothing. As the angels left, at that very moment, the other two women looked up at me and said calmly, "It's done."

I do not pretend to understand all of what went on. This was the only experience I have had like this in my life, and I am near the age of forty. For several months, I kept in contact with the woman for whom we prayed, and there seems to have been a real change in her after this experience. The release she had longed for finally came.

My friend had an angel encounter of the fourth kind. Her angel appeared face to face, which is the exception, not the rule. More on what angels look like a little later in this chapter, but let's back up a bit.

How do you know if an angel has crossed your path? Sometimes you don't, because angels often appear as coincidences. That is, they *seem* like chance events, but they are really part of God's carefully orchestrated plan for your life.

ANGELS OF COINCIDENCE

Genesis 24 is the account of how Abraham found a wife for his son Isaac—"by chance." At the time, Abraham was living on foreign soil, some distance from his kin, so he commissioned his servant, "Go to my country and my own relatives and get a wife for my son Isaac."

The servant asked him, "What if the woman is unwilling to come back with me to this land? (Good question!) Shall I then take your son back to the country you came from?"

"Make sure that you do not take my son back there," Abraham said. "The Lord, the God of heaven, who brought me out of my father's household and my native land and who spoke to me and promised me on oath, saying, 'To your offspring I will give this land'—*he will send his angel before you so that you can get a wife for my son from there*" (Gn 24:1-7, italics mine).

This is the only mention of angels in the text, but I have to believe that Abraham was not just giving his servant a kind of ancient farewell, like, "Angels will go with you, my friend." No, God's angel was working invisibly to bring about answers to prayer. When the servant reached the town of Nahor, he had his camels kneel down near the well outside the town. It was toward evening, the time the women went out to draw water.

The point of all these details is that none of this is accidental. The angel was hard at work as the servant prayed, "O Lord,

God of my master Abraham, give me success today... See, I am standing beside this spring, and the daughters of the townspeople are coming out to draw water. May it be that when I say to a girl, 'Please let down your jar that I may have a drink,' and she says, 'Drink, and I'll water your camels too'—let her be the one you have chosen for your servant Isaac....' Before he had finished praying, Rebekah came out with her jar on her shoulder."

The rest, as they say, is history. One thing led to another. Or maybe we should say an angel was responsible for one thing after another. And Rebekah became Isaac's wife.

For the Christian, there is no such thing as chance events. Every life situation has providential overtones. Maybe it's actually invisible heavenly beings intervening directly on our behalf. My friend, Duane Rawlins, credits an invisible angelic presence for preventing a serious automobile accident.

The incident occurred when I was seventeen years old, a new driver who loved speeding down country roads. It was around 8:00 P.M. one dark evening. Just ahead of me, at the limits of my bright headlights, was a slight rise in the road. A thought flashed in my mind, "I'm going to use that little hill in the road ahead to make this car fly." What I didn't know is that the little hill, which I was approaching at high speed, was a railroad crossing. My vision was blocked by trees, and there was no crossing gate or warning device.

As I lurched up the gentle incline, an unexplainable force suddenly stopped my car—just as an unseen fast train roared over the crossing! The adrenalin of fear raced through my body as I realized what had just happened. I became so weak with fright, I could hardly drive home. I have no doubt that I would have been killed instantly had it not been for that "unexplainable force."

I've collected several reports like this. Here's another, from a member of our church.

One time I was driving in my truck and listening to an Amy Grant cassette. In a heart-stopping moment, I narrowly missed hitting another vehicle head on. "How did we ever miss each other!" I thought to myself.

Within seconds of passing the other car, my Amy Grant cassette popped over on its own to the other side of the tape—my cassette player had this feature—and guess what song I heard? "Angels Watchin' Over Me"!

Maybe that was coincidence, but I chose to believe that it was God's way of saying he was watching over me!

Most angel activity, like this, is invisible. Other times, angels appear disguised as humans—"angels unawares"—something I will discuss and illustrate in a later chapter. But once or twice every few lifetimes[2] angels materialize, literally, in their heavenly forms, much as the two angels appeared to my friend in the story at the beginning of this chapter.

AN ANGEL'S VIEW: ON WINGS AND OTHER THINGS

When angels appear, and when they are not disguised as "chance" events or human beings, what do they look like? In preparation for writing this book, and as a part of my final project for a Doctor of Ministry degree from Western Conservative Baptist Seminary, Phoenix, I conducted a survey[3] of several hundred people in different church settings, including evangelical, charismatic Protestants, and Roman Catholics. Among those who claim to have seen an angel, some aspects of angelic appearances are fairly common.

Of the many angel experiences I collected, perhaps as many as a hundred, the similarities are striking. This is especially significant in that the people who told me their stories did not talk to one another first. They didn't even know each other!

One description stands out as a good example of many of the common elements that appear in many angel encounters. The angels that appeared to one gentleman I surveyed "had arms, hands, legs, feet and wings, and I could see their faces. The figures were full-bodied, transparent and bright. They also seemed to be dressed in a long robes, or something covering them from their necks down to their ankles and their wrists. And they had some type of tie around their waists."

Here's another angel story that is "typical," from a friend, Robert Obergfoll.

It was about ten o'clock when my brother and I, both children at the time, kneeled down beside our beds to pray. From what I can remember, it was a tranquil spring night, the sky bright in the aura of a crescent moon. Our bedroom window faced toward the east, and a slight breeze was making its way through the screen. It was like the curtains were breathing. Gently inhaling. Exhaling.

My brother was in bed first. It was a big night. He had put his tooth under his pillow in preparation for the "tooth fairy." We didn't believe in the tooth fairy business, but as Catholic boys, we believed in angels! So innocently praying that God would send one of his angels to take my brother's tooth, we drifted off to sleep.

Later that night—I have no idea what time it was—a wild wind in our room awakened me. My bed was on the right side of the window, and my brother's bed was on the left. I can still see him sleeping there across the small space between our beds, the stiff breeze whipping the drapes like flags flying parallel to the ground.

Wide-eyed, I stared out the window as a bright light appeared. Suddenly, an angel, as if riding the wind, flew through the window into our bedroom. The angel was standing up straight, as if it had come right through the wall. It was taller than my parents and was as high as the ceiling of our room. It was light blue and transparent. I couldn't tell if it was male or female, but it had long hair and a beautiful face.

The angel never looked at me, but fixed its attention on my

brother, just as we had prayed earlier in the evening. Placing one knee on my brother's bed, the angel stooped down and with his right hand touched him gently on the face.

My first thought was that the angel was going to take his tooth! But it seemed to have another purpose. Without looking at me or even acknowledging that I was in the room, the angel stood up and left our bedroom just as he had come in. The whole experience seemed to take several minutes, but I really have no idea how long it was. After the angel left, I went over and awakened by brother to tell him what happened. We both sat in a moment of stunned awe before going to tell our parents.

Later that same year, my brother was diagnosed with a serious blood disorder. He is alive today, and I believe it is directly related to the touch of that angel.

There are uncanny similarities in my collection of accounts of angel appearances—especially in the descriptions of the angels themselves. They are almost always very tall, usually around ten feet. They are bright, glowing white, often with a slight bluish tint. Their faces are indescribable, so their gender is unrecognizable.[4] They are usually dressed in a full-length robe and frequently girded with a belt or sash of gold.

Unless they are appearing as human beings, which seems to be the case in many of the accounts I heard, angels are transparent. Many people told me the angel they saw was "see-through." Angel appearances are also very brief, and if the angel speaks, it's not usually in the form of normal conversation. It would probably be more accurate to say that angels "communicate" rather than "talk." And, last but not least, in the reports I've been told, the angels do *not* usually have wings!

Is this really what angels look like? Can we depend on what people tell us from their personal experiences? Billy Graham reminds us that "The history of virtually all nations and cultures reveals some belief in angelic beings.... But no matter what the traditions, our frame of reference must be the Scripture as our supreme authority on this subject.[5]

What can we learn from the Bible about angels and how they appear? God's Word suggests three broad categories. *First,* the cherubim. These are a unique class of angels whose appearance and features are given in the most detail in the Bible. We'll talk about the cherubim more in a later chapter. Cherubim, by the way, do have wings.

Second, in the historical books of the Old Testament, nearly every reference to angels is somehow related to "the angel of the Lord," who tends to show up as a man, or an unexpected visitor. In this case, I think "show up" is more accurate than "appear," because that's what he did. The angel of the Lord took on the form of a visitor or guest, who arrived as if he had been on a journey.[6] According to the Bible, the angel of the Lord *never* has wings.

Third, the angel of the Lord is unlike many of the angels in the angelic encounters in the New Testament, where heavenly messengers materialize and then vanish, much like light suddenly appears and disappears in a bulb when you turn the switch on and off. What the angels actually looked like in these appearances is not, in most cases, spelled out in much detail. For example, when the angel Gabriel appears to Zechariah and later Mary in Luke 1, what he looked like is left out completely. No wings. No halos. Not even a beam of light, which is unusual.

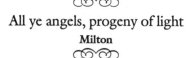

All ye angels, progeny of light
Milton

When angels appeared in the Bible, it seems that radiance or luminescence is their most frequently mentioned trait. This is probably the underlying reason why we almost always see halos in pictures of angels. Halos, of course, are those funny little round, golden crowns, hovering like Saturn's rings a few inches above the heads of angels and holy people in old paintings. Sometimes halos are called "auras."[7]

The presence of God often appeared in the Bible as a luminous cloud—the glory of Yahweh—and angels as messengers seem to be bearers of God's blazing glory, something the Hebrews called "the *shekinah*." In fact, in extraordinary moments, the light of God's special presence can envelop us, too. One time while I was preaching, someone in the congregation reported seeing a haze of light around my body as I spoke. I later wondered about the significance of that event—once is not very often in over twenty years of preaching!

Moses had a similar, albeit much more powerful, encounter with the light of God's presence. After spending time alone with Yahweh on Mount Sinai, Moses' face was so brilliant that the children of Israel could not talk to him without sunglasses. We read about this in Exodus 34:29-30:

> When Moses came down from Mount Sinai with the two tablets of the Testimony in his hands, he was not aware that his face was radiant because he had spoken with the Lord. When Aaron and all the Israelites saw Moses, his face was radiant, and they were afraid to come near him.

Angels, then, are beings of dazzling, sometimes blinding, light, suggesting that their home is in heaven in the bright, resplendent presence of God. Something of God has rubbed off on them.

The light of God and of his angels may have some scientific significance as well. Some have speculated that light, as understood in the framework of Einstein's theory of relativity, is actually the boundary between time and eternity. We know from Einstein's hypothesis and other subsequent experimentation that, as physical matter approaches the speed of light, time slows down and mass becomes infinite. In other words, at the speed of light something extraordinary happens: time and space reality, as we know it, disappears.

The speed of light may represent the boundary of the time and space dimension, a shimmering curtain between the visible, material world and eternity. Perhaps there is a connection here with the biblical affirmation of the nature of deity: God is light.

And maybe this is why angels appear brightly illuminated.

According to many studies of "near-death experiences" (NDEs), dying people, those who are standing on the threshold of timelessness, commonly see a "being of light." Even the resurrection of Christ was accompanied by radiant beings. Matthew reported that "There was a violent earthquake, for an angel of the Lord came down from heaven and, going to the tomb [of Jesus], rolled back the stone and sat on it. *His appearance was like lightning, and his clothes were white as snow*" (Mt 28:2-3, italics mine).

Luke adds, "On the first day of the week, very early in the morning, the women took spices they had prepared and went to the tomb. They found the stone rolled away from the tomb, but when they entered, they did not find the body of the Lord Jesus. While they were wondering about this, suddenly two men *in clothes that gleamed like lightning* stood beside them" (Lk 24:1-4, italics mine).

Angels are heavenly beings, "stars" radiating with the light of God's presence. Hebrews 1:7 calls them "flames of fire," an image "illuminated brilliantly" throughout the Book of Revelation:

> Then I saw another mighty angel coming down from heaven. He was robed in a cloud, with a rainbow [a halo, a multicolored aura of light] above his head; *his face was like the sun, and his legs were like fiery pillars.*   **Revelation 10:1**

> After this I looked and in heaven the temple....Out of the temple came the seven angels with the seven plagues. *They were dressed in clean, shining linen and wore golden sashes around their chests.*   **Revelation 15:5-6 (italics mine)**

> After this I saw another angel coming down from heaven. He had great authority, *and the earth was illuminated by his splendor.*   **Revelation 18:1, (italics mine)**

And then there are the flaming swords. "After he drove the man out, he placed on the east side of the Garden of Eden

And then there are the flaming swords. "After he drove the man out, he placed on the east side of the Garden of Eden cherubim, *and a flaming sword flashing back and forth* to guard the way to the tree of life" (Gn 3:24, italics mine).

My friend, whose account I shared at the beginning of this chapter, saw an angel with a flaming sword of protection and defense standing over the woman who was "giving birth."

What else can we say about how angels look? In the Bible, many of God's heavenly creatures have wings. In Daniel 9:21 we read of an angel who hurried to bring God's message to the prophet. While Daniel was still in prayer, Gabriel came to him "in swift flight" about the time of the evening sacrifice. Wings are not mentioned specifically here, but Daniel's angel must have some aeronautical capabilities!

How sweetly did they float upon the wings
Of silence through the empty-vaulted night.
Milton, *Comus*

Angels can fly because they take
themselves lightly.
Scottish saying

Theodora Ward, in her book *Men and Angels*, observes that "every mythology has winged beings....The association of wings with angels has been so usual that as late as the 1930s the *Shorter Oxford English Dictionary* defined the word 'wing' as 'one of the limbs or organs by which the flight of a bird, bat, insect, *angel*, etc., is affected.'"[9]

Wings, yes. Feathers, no. Nowhere does the Bible suggest that angel wings have feathers, or that they look like bird wings, as they do in so many paintings and sculptures. In fact, for the most part, only the cherubim, a special class of angels, are

wooden sculptures of angels fastened on either end of the atonement cover—the lid—of the Ark of the Covenant.

A small, desk-sized box, fashioned of wood and overlaid with
gold, the Ark (not Noah's ark!) was Yahweh's dwelling place. It
was kept in the small, inner sanctuary called the Holy of Holies
in the tent-like tabernacle of Moses. Between the two golden
cherubim hovered the glory cloud of God's special presence, the
shekinah. Once a year, the high priest, on Yom Kippur—the Day
of Atonement—sprinkled the sacrificial blood on the atonement
cover to redeem Israel from their sins. "The [golden] cherubim
had their wings spread upward, overshadowing the cover with
them. The cherubim faced each other, looking toward the
cover" (Ex 37:9).

Real winged cherubim appear in wondrous glory in Ezekiel.
By this time in Jewish history, Jerusalem and its temple had been
destroyed by the Babylonians, who carried away the Ark and its
golden cherubim as plunder of war. But the *heavenly* cherubim
of Yahweh were still watching over Israel, as Ezekiel found out:

> The appearance of the living creatures [cherubim[10]] was like
> burning coals of fire or like torches. Fire moved back and forth
> among the creatures; it was bright, and lightning flashed out
> of it. The creatures sped back and forth like flashes of light-
> ning.... Spread out above the heads of the living creatures was
> what looked like an expanse, sparkling like ice, and awesome.
> Under the expanse *their wings* were stretched out one toward
> the other, and each had *two wings* covering its body.
>
> Ezekiel 1:13-14, 22-23 (italics mine)

All angels, then, have some means of flight. Some of them
have wings. We also know that angels speak, because they are
regularly talking to people in the Bible. From ancient Jewish
sources, like *Targum Yerushalmi* and *The Book of Jubilee*, we are
told that the language of God at creation and in Eden was
Hebrew. We don't know this from the Bible, but Hebrew is the

language of the Genesis account of creation. Perhaps we could presume the angels spoke the same language.[11]

We also suspect that they speak their own language or languages in heaven. Or maybe they are multilingual. The apostle Paul referred to "the tongues of men *and of angels* (1 Cor 13:1)," indicating that there may be unique heavenly dialects.

Angels even show emotions! In Luke 15:10 Jesus tells us, "There is rejoicing among the angels of God over one sinner whose heart is changed" (Lk 15:10, PHILLIPS). My uncle actually heard this happen once.

In 1967, a friend of his, Joe (not his real name), had recently become a Christian. Having come from a Jewish background, Joe had a high degree of uncertainty about what was happening to him, so he asked God for some kind of sign at his water baptism service.

My uncle and his wife were standing with a small group of Christians on the bank of the Chagrin River, just east of Cleveland, Ohio. No one else was around. No homes were nearby. There was no natural explanation for what happened next.

As Joe was being baptized, for just a few moments, my uncle *and everyone else—including Joe*—heard ethereal music coming right out of the sky. It was unlike anything my uncle had heard before, he told me.

Two years later, in 1969, my uncle and his wife attended their first charismatic praise service, where he heard what charismatics refer to as "singing in the Spirit." When he heard it, he said to himself, "That's like the ethereal music we heard at Joe's baptism!"

Angels were rejoicing in heaven!

But what do angels *do*? We're getting to that in the next chapter.

CHAPTER FOUR

What Good Angels Do for a Living

These are called pure and blessed spirits;
they live upon the earth,
and are good; they watch over mortal men
and defend them from evil;
they keep watch over lawsuits and hard dealings:
they mentor themselves in dark mist
and wander all over the country;
they bestow wealth; for this is right.

Hesiod, *Works and Days*

Angels are ministers and dispensers of the divine bounty toward us. Accordingly, we are told how they watch for our safety, how they undertake our defense, direct our path, and take heed that no evil befall us. **John Calvin**

Why are there angels? Why does God need them—or us? In a certain sense, if God is God, then there *must* be free-will beings. There *must* be angels. God is the ultimate team player, starting with his very nature: he's three Persons existing and working as One God. It's almost as though angels—and human beings—are the necessary creative expressions of the nature of God. Now I don't mean to imply by this that God couldn't control himself when he created the angels and Adam and Eve, that angel life and human life were somehow the inevitable consequence of heavenly evolution. But because God is the way he is, he wouldn't have it any other way. He created human persons and angels to partner with him in his created order.

God doesn't "need" angels, but he uses them! So when things happen mysteriously to shape our lives, is it God or is it an angel?

Yes!

Karl Barth wrote, "We avoid both the over-estimation of angels on the one side and their under-estimation on the other. We contend for the sole lordship and glory of God, but we contend for the lordship and glory of God through the ministry of angels."[1]

Let's talk about what angels actually do for a living.

IT'S ANGELS, FOR HEAVEN'S SAKE!

Most angel work is done in heaven. I've already pointed out that, though there are probably millions of angels who are busy day and night watching over us, most of their work is invisible, and perhaps most of their efforts never touch the earth. Yes, angels minister to the saints—we'll get to this in just a bit—but before anything else, they minister to God.

Praise him, all his angels, praise him, all his heavenly hosts!
Psalm 148:2

Mortimer Adler writes,

> The action of angels on earth and in relation to human beings is, in fact, performed only by *some* angels, not by *all*, not even by *most*. In the main, the life of angels—of *all* angels, even those who carry messages to mankind or have earthly missions to perform—consists in what they do in heaven, not what they do on earth.[2]

This statement may be difficult to prove statistically, but we know this: if angels were created *before* the six days of creation in Genesis, then they must have a higher purpose than "earth work." Or, if not a higher purpose, *other* purposes. Throughout the Bible angels are seen attending to God and serving him. They are agents of God's will, filling heaven with worship and praise:

> Then I looked and heard the voice of many angels, numbering thousands upon thousands, and ten thousand times ten thousand. They encircled the throne and the living creatures [the cherubim] and the elders. In a loud voice they sang: "Worthy is the Lamb, who was slain, to receive power and wealth and wisdom and strength and honor and glory and praise!"
>
> **Revelation 5:11-12**

A woman in our church wrote to me:

> I had an experience with angels during my first year as a Christian. I was praising and worshiping for several hours— no distractions whatsoever. It was a tremendous experience. Suddenly, in the middle of a song, I heard many, many voices sing together with me. I didn't see any angels, and there wasn't any music playing. It was just singing voices!

Angels minister to God with praise and worship. Angels ministered to Jesus, too, and though they relate in similar ways to us, perhaps we can feel the special affinity the angels have for the Son of God. Although we know from Scripture that angels are not direct heirs of salvation, certainly they must have known something of the story of redemption as God sent his Son into the world. They surely understood something of the solemn and grand purpose for which God had become incarnate.

After all, while shepherds were watching their flocks by night, angels announced the birth of the Savior with a heavenly concert. And after Jesus' prolonged temptation in the wilderness, they ministered to him. Mark reported in his Gospel, "At once the Spirit sent him out into the desert, and he was in the desert forty days, being tempted by Satan. He was with the wild animals, *and angels attended him*" (Mk 1:12-13, italics mine).

EIGHT KINDS OF ANGELIC WORK

The primary work of angels, then, is in heaven, ministering to God. Secondarily, angels work in time and space, a labor which falls into at least eight broad categories.

Angels are messengers. They bring good tidings (see Luke 2:10). As I wrote in an earlier chapter, message-bearing is a basic function of angels, implied by the very meaning of the biblical terms *malak* and *angelos*, both which mean "messenger." Sometimes the message is just good news. Other times it's prophetic, about somebody's future—or the future of the whole world.

In the first two chapters of Revelation, seven "angels" are sent to the seven churches of Asia Minor. Each angel bears a message of encouragement and correction, targeted for the unique situation in each of the churches. Bible scholars have debated the identity of these angels. It is not certain if the *angelos* of each church refers to some prophetic person, the local pastor, or an actual heavenly angel. Since real angels play such a large role in Revelation—you can find them in every chapter but one—I am inclined to believe that the "angels of the seven churches" are angels. This would suggest that God assigns special message-bearing angels to local churches.

How their messages to the churches are communicated, however, is not clear. Each of the seven messages of Revelation chapters 2 and 3 ends with the phrase, "He that has an ear to hear, let him hear what the Spirit [not the angel] is saying to the churches." The Spirit of God speaks. He is the source of the message. Angels, then, carry the message, and it's delivered, perhaps, by the local church leader or by respected, spiritually sensitive people in each local church.

I believe, partly from my own experience (angels have appeared when I am preaching), that those who have positions of leadership in the church—apostles, prophets, evangelists, pastors, teachers, elders, and others—are the object of a special angelic presence, especially when they are doing the work of the ministry. I cannot "prove" this from Scripture, but if the body of Christ is the expression of God's kingdom power in the earth,[3] then it follows that angelic presence and power are allied with the authority of the church. God's power and angelic power are standing with us as we stand for Christ and advance his kingdom purposes on the earth.

I must add, of course, that God's authority, including the support of his angels, is related to human leaders only as they are doing the will of God. In other words, sooner or later God will lift angelic power, protection, and blessing from those who are adulterating their calling.

In another example of messenger angels, Gabriel appeared two times in Luke 1, first to the Jewish priest Zechariah—with a long prophecy about the unlikely birth of his son, John the Baptist; and later to Mary—about the even more unlikely birth of her son, Jesus (Lk 1:5-25, 26-38). And in a slightly different role, herald angels—some angel messages are more like announcements—will trumpet the Second Coming of Christ:

> For the Lord himself will come down from heaven, with a
> loud command, with the voice of the archangel and with the

trumpet of God, and the dead in Christ will rise first. After that, we who are still alive and are left will be caught up together in the clouds to meet the Lord in the air.

1 Thessalonians 4:16-17

The "quick and the dead" will hear the voice of the archangel. Angels were also present to herald the resurrection of Christ:

The angel said to the women, "Do not be afraid, for I know that you are looking for Jesus, who was crucified. He is not here; he has risen, just as he said. Come and see the place where he lay."

Matthew 28:5-7

The angel announced the resurrection, but there's more. There's direct guidance: "Go quickly and tell his disciples: 'He has risen from the dead.'"

Earlier in Jesus' life, during his childhood, an angel appeared to Joseph in a dream, instructing him to flee with Mary and the Child to Egypt. "Herod," the angel said, "is going to search for the child to kill him" (Mt 2:13).

Probably every angel message contains some form of guidance, but some messages are more specific, like the ones illustrated by the Bible verses above. It's always important to remember, however, that spiritual guidance, whatever shape it takes, even if it's from an angel, must be carefully submitted to the Scriptures and wise counsel before we make any serious life changes. This is especially crucial when our decisions affect other people. Never forget that there are good angels who lead us while evilangels love to lead us astray.

Wendy Reece shared with me her story of good guidance from a good angel.

When I was about sixteen years old, my sister and I shared the same bedroom. One night, in the middle of the night, after we had both fallen asleep, I was abruptly awakened by a bright light. I thought someone had turned on the bedroom light! I saw my sister asleep in her bed across the room—with her back turned toward me.

Suddenly, I saw a "being" or person standing in front of me. His back was towards my sister. He was very tall and wearing an ivory robe. I don't remember seeing his face closely, because I was looking up to him. I do remember that the face reminded me of pictures I'd seen of Jesus—long, brownish-red hair and a beard.

I looked over at my sister, but she remained asleep. I remember feeling calm and wondering if I was just having a very vivid dream. I knew I was awake, though. This angel, this vision, or whatever, didn't stay long, but he did speak to me briefly. I don't remember any exact words, but he said that sometime, when I would be in my twenties, I would experience terrible tragedy. *But...* he wanted me to know that Jesus would be there for me. With that big little message, he then disappeared. And the light in the room went off.

When I woke up the next morning, I was sure I had just had a vivid dream and never told anyone about it. Naturally, it worried me, but I just didn't think about it for several years.

But in February, 1987, some ten years later (I was twenty-seven, in the Air Force in Germany), my brother called in the middle of the night to tell me my father had just died of a heart attack—at the age of forty-eight.

I flew home to Ohio for the funeral, and after a very difficult time, returned to Germany. My mother visited me that summer. She was so depressed. I did not know how to cope with her grief or my own. You see, even though I had seen an angel, I was not a Christian at the time.

Just two weeks after my mother returned to the states, I got another phone call. This time it was my mother. Just like my dad, she died of a heart attack at forty-eight. And then that fall my husband left me.

Before asking Christ into my life, I would often lie on my bed weeping and crying out over and over, "Jesus, help me!"

while I clung to a crucifix necklace I wore. I really did not understand how I could open my life to Jesus, and how his Holy Spirit could change me inside.

But he heard my desperate pleas. It was no accident that I was reunited with a close friend who had become a Christian since the last time we were together. I can't find words to describe how wonderfully she helped me with her prayers and loving support. She took me to a Women's Aglow Bible study where I accepted Jesus as my personal Savior.

While praying with some other Christians, I remembered the angel who appeared to me when I was sixteen, and I realized that what I was told had been true: I would face a terrible time in my twenties, but Jesus had been there for me and would never leave me or forsake me.

Angels are bearers of God. Second, angels do more than bring messages. They bring something of God's presence with them. Angels are not intimidating just because they are awesome spiritual beings. People often fall down before them because they come directly from the presence of God. I touched on this earlier in the book when I discussed the glory of God that rubs off on angels and people who are near him. Angel messages are more than just bits and pieces of divine information dropped like propaganda leaflets from heavenly aviators. Angel messages pulsate with the presence of the Lord. Angels are beings of light, and their messages glow with God. Sometimes they don't even have to say anything, but their presence alone communicates clearly the love and protection of God.

Angels bring answers to prayer. A third category of angel labor, very much related to the first two, is that angels somehow assist God in answering our prayers. God, of course, gets all the credit and glory, but angels mysteriously assist in the process. Peter's miraculous deliverance from prison is a case in point. He had been jailed for refusing to stop preaching to the Jewish community about Jesus. In the middle of the night, an angel entered the Roman prison and escorted Peter, much to his amazement, out of his cell into the deserted streets of Jerusalem.

Peter was still pinching himself as the angel disappeared into the night. We find out later in the account that this is all a direct result of the fervent prayers of the early church. When the reality of his escape dawned on Peter, "He went to the house of Mary the mother of John, also called Mark, where many people had gathered and were praying" (Acts 12:12). They could only have been praying about one thing: Peter's safety and release. And an angel engineered it. Sometimes angels bring answers to prayer. Sometimes they *are* the answer!

Angels provide protection and deliverance. Carrying notes from God, however, is not the angels' only labor of love. Angels protect us, intervene on our behalf, and deliver us from dangerous situations. The best known Scripture in this regard is Psalm 91:11, "For he will command his angels concerning you to guard you in all your ways." In the familiar record of Daniel in the den of lions, the king called out to him in an anguished voice, "Servant of the living God, has your God, whom you serve continually, been able to rescue you from the lions?"

Daniel answered, "O king, live forever! My God sent his angel, and he shut the mouths of the lions. They have not hurt me, because I was found innocent in his sight" (Dn 6:20-22).

A whole chapter on guardian angels, with some great personal experiences, awaits you just ahead!

Angels disperse supernatural provision. On several occasions in the Bible, angels provided for the physical needs of people in urgent situations. In Genesis 21, Sarah in a fit of jealousy had her handmaid Hagar—who was also Abraham's concubine—thrown out of the house. Hagar was given provisions and sent out into nowhere. When the water in her leather canteen ran out, she put her little son Ishmael under a bush.

Then she went off and sat down nearby, about a bowshot away, for she thought, "I cannot watch the boy die." And as she sat there she began to sob.

God heard the boy crying, and the angel of God called to Hagar from heaven and said to her, "What is the matter, Hagar? Do not be afraid; God has heard the boy crying as he lies there. Lift the boy up... for I will make him into a great nation."

Then God opened her eyes and she saw a well of water. So she went and filled the skin with water and gave the boy a drink.   **Genesis 21:16-19**

God saved Ishmael's life—and the future of the Arab peoples.

In another Bible passage (1 Kgs 19:1ff), the feisty prophet Elijah, after personally slaughtering four hundred fifty prophets of the pagan god Baal,[4] fled like a coward from the wicked and idolatrous queen Jezebel.

"Elijah was afraid," the Bible tells us in a bit of an understatement, because he "ran for his life." After about a day of running, Elijah sat down under a broom tree and prayed to die. "I have had enough, Lord. Take my life," he moaned, as he fell asleep in his depression.

All at once, the Bible tells us, an angel appeared, touched him and said, "Get up and eat." Elijah looked around, and "there by his head was a cake of bread baked over hot coals, and a jar of water." When he fell asleep a second time, the angel poked him again and said, "Get up and eat, for the journey is too much for you." So Elijah did what the angel commanded and survived forty days on the water and bread from heaven!

Sometimes angels bring messages. Sometimes, they bring lunch. The pastor of our Spanish ministry at our church, Hector Torres, had an angel tell him how to fix his car!

During the summer of 1982, I traveled with my extended family to Colombia, my native land. There were sixteen of us, including parents, brothers, sisters, and grandchildren. One day, we all decided to visit the archaeological ruins of San Augustin in the southwestern part of Columbia, nearly four hundred miles from our family home in Bogotá.

Late in the afternoon, after hours of driving in a desolate, mountainous area, the vehicle I was driving suddenly lost power and the engine died in a feeble sputter. My first thought was that we had run out of gas, but the fuel gauge showed we still had more than half a tank.

Checking under the hood, we could find nothing noticeably wrong. There we were. In the middle of "nowhere," in a totally deserted area. And it was getting dark. My brother Gabriel and I joined hands and began to pray for God's intervention. We prayed in faith that God would not forsake us, that he would provide help in this time of need.

Just as we finished praying, out of nowhere, a Jeep with two passengers drove up and stopped to help. Listening to our story, one of the men said to me, "Get down underneath the gas tank and reconnect the fuel line."

It was almost like Jesus telling Peter to drop his fishing nets on the other side of his boat. I crawled under our car, and sure enough, the fuel line was disconnected. Somehow this "person" knew what was wrong—without looking.

I promptly reconnected the fuel hose and the car started up without a problem! By this time, the two men who had stopped to help us had climbed back into their Jeep and had driven away.

The interesting thing is that, from certain vantage points along that mountain road, the lights of other vehicles could be seen for miles. Yet none of us could see any vehicle lights anywhere ahead of us for the next couple of hours. We actually tried to drive as fast as we could in an attempt to catch up to the people who had helped us. But they were not to be seen again. They just vanished into the night.

When we arrived at the next village, a couple hours after the incident, we looked for the men and their vehicle—and inquired of the townspeople. But no one had seen them. My brother and I believe we had been visited by angels.

Angels are ministering spirits, heavenly pastors. A sixth angel assignment is the ministration of comfort and mercy. Perhaps the best known Scripture in this regard is Hebrews 1:14: "Are not all angels ministering spirits sent to serve those who will inherit salvation?" The Greek term for "ministering," a word from which we get the English "liturgy," refers to service, especially sacred service, doing the service of God. "Ministering angels" are sent "to serve" the saints. In the service of God, angels serve God's people. Perhaps we could say that "to minister to" means simply to care for. Angels care for us according to our needs. They are almost like heavenly pastors.

The look of heaven is on the land and sea,
And something in this pale celestial light
Has loosed my yoke of weariness from me.
Grace Noll Crowell[5]

Angels bring good news and helpful guidance, but as I mentioned earlier in this chapter, what they say is not nearly as significant as how they say it. Angel messages are infused with the presence of God, and God's real presence brings real peace. "May the Lord bless you and keep you," goes the ancient benediction. "May the Lord make his face—his immediate presence—shine upon you and be gracious to you. May the Lord lift up his countenance—his radiant presence—upon you. *And give you peace*" (Nm 6:24-26, my paraphrase).

The Hebrew term for "peace" is, of course, *shalom*, a powerful word which carries with it the idea of everything that God's presence can possibly mean to us. In fact, for the Hebrews, *shalom* is the word that describes the wholeness of the messianic kingdom. The millennium is *shalom*. *Shalom* is heaven.

Heaven comes to people—and their loved ones—when they are dying. It is not uncommon for angels to appear when people are on the edge of death, and people who have had near-death experiences often describe feelings of indescribable peace. Angels. The presence of God. *Shalom.*

LeeAnn Rawlins told me her experience of wonderful angel comfort at the death of her first husband:

> It happened the morning my first husband, Willard, passed away. I didn't know it at the moment, but death was about to end our marriage of twenty-three years.
>
> Willard had been suffering from a terminal illness, and we were alone together in our family room. In pain, my husband groaned, "It hurts." At that very instant, without another warning, Willard went to be with the Lord.
>
> It was such an unusual experience, because in that sad, sad moment, I also felt an awesome, comforting presence enter the room, just as my husband's spirit left him. I did not "see" an angel, but the angel's presence was unmistakable. In a wonderful way that same angel stayed close to me and stood by me and comforted me often during those awful years following Willard's death.

Angels ministered peace to Jesus after his horrible temptation in the wilderness (Mk 1:13). And, under very similar circumstances, an angel ministered comfort and strength to the prophet Daniel, who for three weeks had been in spiritual travail for the release of Israel from her exile in Babylon and alienation from Yahweh. "I ate no choice food," Daniel reported. "No meat or wine touched my lips; and I used no lotions at all until the three weeks were over."

At the end of his fast, a great angel appeared. I should point out that the Bible does not suggest that Daniel's fast *caused* the angel to appear. Angels are not obligated to show themselves to us, no matter how spiritual we are. But in this case, Daniel was waging war in prayer for God's purposes on the earth to unfold. Standing on the bank of the Tigris River in Babylon, Daniel looked up and there before him was "a man dressed in linen, with a belt of the finest gold around his waist. His body was like chrysolite, his face like lightning, his eyes like flaming torches, his arms and legs like the gleam of burnished bronze, and his voice like the sound of a multitude" (Dn 10:1ff).

The angel was very loud. He was extraordinarily powerful too. His hand touched Daniel and, as Daniel tells it, "set me trembling on my hands and knees." Daniel was in the vortex of the powers of heaven and hell, spinning in a swirling moment of time and eternity.

Spiritual warfare is hell. It torments the soul and exhausts the body, for "we wrestle not (the analogy is an appropriate one) against flesh and blood, but with principalities and powers of... darkness" (Eph 6:12 KJV).

Daniel wrote,

> "I am overcome with anguish because of the vision, my lord, and I am helpless. How can I, your servant, talk with you, my lord? My strength is gone and I can hardly breathe."
>
> Again the one who looked like a man touched me and gave me strength. "Do not be afraid, O man highly esteemed," he said. "Peace! [*Shalom!*] Be strong now; be strong."
>
> **Daniel 10:16-19**

The angel ministered to Daniel. Gave him strength. Gave him peace. Gregory of Nyssa wrote, "The Lord of the Angels procures life and peace through the angels for those who are worthy."[6]

Angels help God shape history. Angels are guardians of nations. The idea of angels over cities and geographical territories has only recently been reintroduced in the church, though the idea of regional spirits is as old as the Bible. John Calvin wrote,

> When Daniel introduces the angel of the Persians and the angel of the Greeks (Daniel 10:12-13), he undoubtedly intimates that certain angels are appointed as a kind of precedence over kingdoms and provinces.[7]

In my book on spiritual warfare, *Overcoming the Dominion of Darkness*, I defined evil territorial spirits as "the hierarchy of dark beings that are strategically assigned by Satan himself to influence and control nations, communities, and even families. A multilevel system of spiritual beings is suggested by Ephesians 6:12."[8]

The recent revival of interest in spiritual warfare has rediscovered the reality of the spiritual dimension and the principalities and powers of good and evil that intersect with events here on earth. Angels, dark and light, influence government, economics, and culture—and help shape human history. C. Fred Dickason writes, "Behind the human scene, angels busily exercise influence and engage in battle. Individually or collectively, they may guide the governments of the earth."[9]

I found the unusual account which follows in one of the earliest histories of the church. Eusebius, often known as the father of church history, was carefully studied and followed by a little-known Christian historian by the unlikely name of Socrates. In his *Ecclesiastical History*, Socrates reported an unusual vision of angels during a time of uneasy relations between Constantinople, the capital of Christian civilization, and the Persians. Socrates wrote,

> As the Constantinopolitans were in great consternation, and apprehensive respecting the issue of the war, angels from God appeared to some persons in Bithynia who were traveling to Constantinople on their own affairs, and bade them tell the people not to be alarmed, but pray to God and be assured that the Romans [that is, the people of the Holy Roman Empire, centered in Constantinople] would be conquerors. For they said that they themselves were appointed by God to defend them. When this message was circulated, it not only comforted the residents of the city, but rendered the soldiers more courageous.[10]

I was told of a similar incident when I visited Russia recently. The Russians have a brutal history of invasion and occupation, and the Eastern Orthodox cathedrals were actually used as fortresses of refuge from the cruel Tartar hordes. During a visit to one of those magnificent, vaulted cathedrals, every square inch of its walls painted with brilliant, gilded frescoes, I thought to myself, "This cathedral is ten times more awesome than my personal prayer life. No wonder people are attracted to this."

Ignorantly and perhaps insensitively, I commented to our Russian interpreter, "This place is magnificent! It's no wonder these soaring arches have become a substitute for a personal relationship with God."

With tears welling in her eyes, Kathy rebuked me politely, "Yes," she said, "I understand the importance of a personal relationship with God." She was a born-again Christian. "But these cathedrals are the soul of Russia. The Church brought us education and culture. And these buildings, these great buildings, saved countless Russian lives. People would crowd into places like this and stand shoulder to shoulder, sometimes for days, while the invading Tartars burned and sacked our cities. The invaders *would not*, however, harm our people who had taken refuge in our cathedrals. The invaders feared the retaliation of God if they damaged a church or harmed anyone inside."

Later, another interpreter, also a Christian and a student of Orthodox history, told me a little more of the angelic protection during those awful days. On one occasion, she told me with pride, Tartars retreated wildly from a Russian city when they saw a large angel hovering above the central cathedral.

The same kind of thing happened in the Bible. In an Old Testament passage I referenced earlier in this book, the king of Aram went looking for his adversary Elisha, who was hiding in the town of Dothan. Aram surrounded the city, and Elisha, it appeared, had no way of escaping capture and death. But God was with him. And so were the angels. "Don't be afraid," the prophet reassured his servant. "Those who are with us are more than those who are with them." Then the Lord opened the servant's eyes, and he saw the hills full of horses and chariots of fire—angels, we presume—all around Elisha (2 Kgs 6:13-17).

Angels protected Elisha and delivered him. Angels are

guardians of people, cities and nations. God promised Israel early in their history, "See, I am sending an angel ahead of you to guard you along the way and to bring you to the place I have prepared" (Ex 23:20). And in Daniel 12:1 we read about Michael, a great angel assigned the task of protecting the people of Israel.

Some might argue that these angels have not done a very good job, because millions of Jews have lost their lives in shameful blood baths, some in the name of Christianity. But the bright side is that the Hebrews have accomplished something unparalleled in human history. They have maintained their identity as a people for nearly two thousand years! Without national boundaries or even a general region for a homeland! God has always had a special plan for Israel, and he has dispatched angels like Gabriel to ensure that his plans don't fail.

In fact, God has unique plans for *every* nation, and angels are in those plans, too. Basilea Schlink, whose deeply spiritual books have been sold by the millions, wrote, "From the allusions made in Holy Scripture we may infer that God has divided the vast territory of His kingdom into provinces, which He has entrusted to exalted angelic princes and their domains and areas of administration."[11]

In the last book of the Bible, Revelation, although there is no mention of specific angels governing specific regions, angels nevertheless are often connected with geographical areas. In Revelation 7:1, for example, John saw angels standing at the four corners of the earth, and in 9:14 there are four angels that are somehow bound in the vicinity of the Euphrates River.

Daniel 4 is one of the best biblical examples of angelic intervention in human history. Nebuchadnezzar, King of Babylon, was in for some tough times. "In the visions I saw while lying on my bed, I looked, and there before me was a messenger, a holy one, coming down from heaven. He called in a loud voice: 'Cut down the tree and trim off its branches; strip off its leaves and scatter its fruit. Let the animals flee from under it and the birds from its branches'" (Dan 4:13-14).

The "tree" was a symbol of Nebuchadnezzar's past success—and his fragile future. He was within an eyelash of losing everything because of his pride. God was about to humble him with insanity, ultimately, in order to save him and his kingdom. Who cuts down the tree? God, although the dream doesn't tell us that specifically. But we certainly know who gave the command: "a holy one," *an angel.*

Angels help God shape history. C. Fred Dickason writes, "Behind the human scene, angels busily exercise influence and engage in battle. Individually or collectively they may guide the governments of the earth."[12]

Angels may also be at least partly responsible for some natural disasters. The appearance of angels at the empty tomb was accompanied by an earthquake (Mt 28:2), and in Revelation, angel appearances are repeatedly attended by cataclysmic events on earth. In 7:1, for example, angels are given power over the weather, as they are commanded to hold "back the four winds of the earth to prevent any wind from blowing on the land or on the sea or on any tree." This is the deafening silence just before the huge storm of God's judgment!

And when the judgment came, "The seventh angel poured out his bowl into the air, and out of the temple came a loud voice from the throne, saying, 'It is done.' Then there came flashes of lightning, peals of thunder, and a severe earthquake" (Rv 16:17-18). Now the Bible does not tell here that angels *caused* these phenomena, but somehow they are right in the middle of them. They are participating with God, influencing "natural" events and shaping history.

Good angels bring bad news. Lastly, angels play a significant role in carrying out the judgments of God, especially in the last days and at the end of the world. Not all good angels bring good news. It's not that angels are angry. They're just doing their job. God is the judge, and his angels are the executioners. In fact, the role of the angels in the administration of God's justice is second only to their assignment as messengers. The Bible contains dozens of references to angels of judgment—from death angels assigned the task of taking the life of a single, reprobate individual...

> On the appointed day Herod, wearing his royal robes, sat on his throne and delivered a public address to the people. They shouted, "This is the voice of a god, not of a man." Immediately, because Herod did not give praise to God, an angel of the Lord struck him down, and he was eaten by worms and died.[13]

... to the angels of God's wrath responsible for the punishment of vast numbers of people:

> The third angel sounded his trumpet, and a great star, blazing like a torch, fell from the sky on a third of the rivers and on the springs of water—the name of the star is Wormwood. A third of the waters turned bitter, and many people died from the waters that had become bitter.   **Revelation 8:10-11**

Angels make you want to hide. Sometimes they even make you want to die. And sometimes they just make you die. Good angels always follow through on their assignment to do God's will; that's what makes them good, even if they do the worst imaginable things—like burning up the earth (Rv 8:8) or killing the firstborn of the Egyptians (Ex 12:23).

Paul wrote to the Corinthians, "And do not grumble, as some of them [that is, the Israelites in the wilderness] did—and were killed by the destroying angel" (1 Cor 10:10). Good angels are not always harmless, smiling little cherubs, like Christmas tree ornaments, any more than God is a big ball of cosmic love.

There is a divinely appointed order in the universe, and when it is violated, there's a price to pay. "There is only one Lawgiver and Judge," James writes, "the one who is able to save and destroy" (Jas 4:12).

Paul wrote, "Do not be deceived: God cannot be mocked. A man reaps what he sows. The one who sows to please his sinful nature, from that nature will reap destruction; the one who sows to please the Spirit, from the Spirit will reap eternal life" (Gal 6:7-8).

Angels are not mentioned in this text, but it's clear they participate both in blessing—and cursing. This is important to understand because a dark legion of New Age angels also exists, angels so skilled in deception that you may be led to believe that God is always on your side—no matter what you do. You may even be tricked into thinking that the *angel* is God. If that happens, you will watch with shock and anguish as your future incinerates in the fiery judgment of God's displeasure.

Have you heard the anti-litter slogan of the Lone Star State? *Don't mess with Texas!* Messin' with Texas is nothin' like messin' with God and his angels. Or foolin' around with dark angels in disguise.

SOME THINGS GOOD ANGELS JUST DON'T DO

As we conclude this chapter on what angels do for a living, it might be helpful to spell out some things angels *don't* do, or more precisely, what *good* angels don't do. If an angel *looks* good and does any of the following things, it is *not* good. It's a dark angel in disguise.

Good angels never try to change Scripture. The messages of good angels *never* supersede or contradict the Bible. If they do, they are messages of deception. It is true that significant portions of biblical revelation were delivered by angels—the entire book of Revelation, for example, is probably the result of angelic messages. John tells us that "he [Jesus] made it [the revelation] known *by sending his angel* to his servant John" (Rv 1:1).

Yet that same book pronounces a curse on anyone who adds or takes away from the words of the book (Rv 22:18-19). This indicates clearly that subsequent revelation would always be subject to biblical authority. In our day, God continues to lead us, to speak to us, to give us a deeper understanding of himself and his ways, but God is finished adding to the Bible.

Good angels refuse to be worshipped. Respected? Yes. Adored like God? Never. Very early in church history, Origen wrote, "We find that because [angels] are divine they are sometimes termed 'god' in the sacred Scriptures, but not so that we are commanded to honour and worship—in place of God— those who minister to us, and bear to us His blessings."[14]

Nor are angels objects of prayer. Angels may help God answer prayer, but never does the Bible suggest that we direct our intercession to any heavenly beings other than God. Good angels never draw attention to themselves. They can sure get your attention, but they it do for God's sake, not theirs.

In the grand scheme of things, angels are positioned somewhere between God and man, but this does not mean they are intermediaries. My personal secretary, at times, speaks for me. She's my "messenger" to the church staff and to people in the congregation. In that sense, she's "between" me and our other ministers, but in no sense is she "over" them. She has authority as my representative, but her position is not higher in the chain of command of our organization than the other people who work for me.

No person in the Bible ever initiates conversation with an angel. People talk to angels, but angels always talk first. New Age angels—dark angels—are different. You can talk to them like you call a friend on the phone; they're just waiting for you to ask them to serve you. The authors of *Ask Your Angels*, for example, tell us confidently, "People in our [angel] workshops are amazed at how easy it is to talk with their angels.... Now that you have mastered the first three steps [something they call Grounding, Releasing, and Aligning] in opening to your angel, you are prepared to speak directly to your celestial friend." Your personal angel is right there to lead you.

Good angels are right there, too. They are probably nearby as you read this book. But good angels don't answer the call of the saints. Only God does that. Anyone who tells you that you can talk to your angel is giving you advice that contradicts the Word of God. They may also be inviting you to entertain the angels of hell.

Angels are not omnipotent, omniscient, or omnipresent. In other words, angels are not all-powerful, although they are very powerful. Angels are not all-knowing, although they seem to be highly intelligent. Angels are not everywhere at once, although they are faster than jets in getting from one place to another. Angels are godlike, but next to God they are like flashlights on the surface of the sun.

Angels do not violate the free will of humans. Angels play a very active role in the purposes of God and the affairs of men, but do not control human events or violate the free will of human beings. Sophy Burnham writes:

> In the High Middle Ages, angels were considered to govern the four elements of earth, air, water, and fire. They moved the stars, tended plants, and graced the procreation of all living creatures, including the births of human kind. Each day of the week had a protecting angel, each season, each astrological sign, each hour of the day or night. In fact, everything you ever thought of or did or wrote or watched was governed by an angel of its own.[15]

Unlike the superstitious men and women whose opinions prevailed in the Middle Ages, we must recognize that God continues to use his angels to guide us, but not to control our environment; to teach us, but not to dictate to us; to protect us, but not to violate the free will he bestowed upon us at Creation. Angels are not moving every leaf on a thousand trees on a windy day.

CHAPTER FIVE

Your Personal Angel

Angels, where e're we go,
Attend our steps whate'er betide.
With watchful care their charge
    attend,
And evil turn aside.

Charles Wesley

Among the angels, some are set in charge of nations, others are companions of the faithful.

St. Basil

Guardian angels are perhaps the most popular kind, probably because we all know how fragile life can be—how little control we seem to have over the events that shape our lives. We desperately need protection from unexpected circumstances and unseen dangers. Just the thought of good angels hovering around us gives people a feeling of safety!

A LITTLE HISTORY

The idea of guardian angels was fairly well developed in Judaism around the time in which the New Testament was written. According to Colin Brown, Judaism taught that each individual had his or her own personal angel,[1] a view generally attested to by the records of the early church. The great preacher Chrysostom, in his *Homilies on Colossians,* affirmed that "each believer hath an angel."[2]

In the third century, Gregory Thaumaturgus wrote to Origen, "But we, in addition to the homage we offer to the Common Ruler of all men, acknowledge and praise that being [the guardian angel], whoever he is, who has been the wonderful guide of our childhood, who in all other matters has been in time past my beneficent tutor and guardian."[3]

Origen, one of the best known writers of early Christian history, wrote, "All the faithful in Christ, no matter how small, are helped by an angel, and Christ says that these angels always see the face of the Father who is in heaven.... We must say that every human soul is under the direction of an angel who is like a father."[4]

St. Basil believed that "an angel is put in charge of every believer, provided we do not drive him out by sin. He guards the soul like an army."[5] And Saint Bernard of Clairvaux grew most eloquent whenever writing or speaking about our guardian angels:

> O wonderful condescension of God! O love true marvelous!... The Most High has commanded the angels, his angels, those sublime spirits, so blessedly happy and so near his throne, his familiar, his closest friends. He has given his angels charge over you. Who are you? *What is man, that you art mindful of him?...* And what do you think he has ordered them to do for your sake?—To protect you.[6]

The early church father Eusebius wrote, "Fearing lest sinful mankind should be without government and without guidance, *like herds of cattle,* God gave them protectors and superintendents, the holy angels, in the form of captains and shepherds. His First-Born Son is set above all these."[7]

It is quite evident from these and other sources that, within the first few centuries of church history, Christians believed that every man and woman, and especially every child, had a personal guardian angel, an idea still generally held by Catholics today.

One Catholic writer, Jean Danielou, affirms confidently, "*Beyond a doubt*, this is a doctrine which appears in Scripture ... that every believer has an angel to guide him as a teacher and a shepherd."[8] Catholic children are still taught that a good angel sits on your right shoulder and a bad one on your left, and you get to choose between the two at every moment of your life.[9]

Expounding this view of the angels, Gregory of Nyssa wrote,

> After our nature had fallen in sin, we were not abandoned in our fall by God, but an angel, one of the beings who have incorporeal nature, was set up to aid the life of each of us. The destroyer of our nature, in his turn, did just the same by sending us an evil, pernicious angel to the detriment of human nature. It now depends upon man, who finds himself between two angels, each one seeking to lead him in a different way, to make the one triumph over the other. The good angel presents his spirit with the fruits of virtue, everything that those who do good see in hope. The other angel holds up before him the pleasures of earth, pleasures which hold no hope for the future, but pleasures which can captivate the minds of the foolish when they are seen and enjoyed in the present.[10]

Jean Danielou asserts, "It is true that an angel has been given to each man at birth. That is a [Catholic] doctrine of long standing."[11] Catholic angelology, Danielou says, is based on Genesis 48:16, Matthew 18:10 (which we will look at a little later), and Tobias 3:25. The Book of Tobias, one of the fourteen apocryphal books which appear at the end of the Old Testament in Catholic Bibles,[12] is not included in Protestant Bibles. This is why many Protestants would argue that Catholic angelology is not purely biblical.

Another Catholic writer, Pascal Parente, tells us, "The often-mentioned activity of the Archangel Raphael, in favor of old Tobias and his son, is the best illustration of the manifold duties of a Guardian Angel. The entire book *Tobias* gives us not only an example of patience and charity in the holy man Tobias, but also reveals to us the wonderful and loving ministry of our Guardian Angels."[13]

Exacting Protestants would wholeheartedly support the idea of guardian angels, that a major role of the angels is to protect the saints. But they would not all agree that every individual has a personal angel. Nor do Protestants teach—because this is even harder if not impossible to find in the Bible—"the doctrine of the two ways," the idea that "all men are moved by two angels, an evil one who inclines them to evil and a good one who inclines them to good."[14]

John Calvin wrote, "Whether each of the faithful has a particular angel assigned him for his defense, I cannot venture certainly to affirm." He conceded that certain angels are charged with the safety of children, based on the well-known statement in Matthew 18:10, but Calvin didn't think that this verse "justifies the conclusion that every one of them has a particular guardian angel." Calvin preferred to think that "not one angel only has the care of every one of us, but that all the angels together with one consent watch over our salvation."[15]

A LITTLE BIBLE

The Bible says less about personal guardian angels than you might think. Of the several hundred references to angels in the Scriptures, only a handful suggest that people have angels assigned to watch over them.[16] I don't mean to imply by this that angels guard us only occasionally, or that this is not really important in the Bible. It's just that what we emphasize about angels is not always what the Bible emphasizes.

Probably the best known Bible verse about guardian angels is

Psalm 91:11, which the devil used to tempt Jesus to act presumptuously: "For he will command his angels concerning you to guard you in all your ways; they will lift you up in their hands, so that you will not strike your foot against a stone." Jesus did not fall for the trap. He overcame the Evil One by the Word of the Lord.

Our lesson here is that God doesn't send his angels just to compensate for our impertinence. Angels are all around us, though, to protect us from untimely calamities. Psalm 34:7 assures us, "The angel of the Lord encamps around those who fear him, and he delivers them."

One of my favorite Bible passages about guardian angels is in Acts 12, a passage to which I referred briefly in the last chapter. Early in the history of the Christian movement, Herod arrested some of the key leaders of the church. "He had James, the brother of John, put to death with the sword." (Remember that, because we are coming back to this passionless report of James' death. It's an important part of what the Bible teaches us about angels.) "When [Herod] saw that this pleased the Jews, he proceeded to seize Peter also."

The night before his trial, Peter, bound with chains, was sleeping between two soldiers, and "sentries stood guard at the entrance." In other words, his arrest was well-secured, and there wasn't a flicker of hope that he could escape.

Suddenly an angel appeared, lighting the cell. He hit Peter on the side, the Bible tells us. "Quick, get up!" he said, and as the chains fell off Peter's wrists, the angel added, "And you better get dressed." Lights came on. The angel was talking. Chains were clinking. Peter was shuffling around getting dressed. Yet the guards kept snoring! This was the other half of the miracle.

Still trying to blink the sleep out of his eyes, Peter followed the angel out of the prison. Passing by two other guards and watching the prison gate swing open of its own accord, Peter found himself standing in the dark street outside the prison.

As the angel vanished, Peter finally realized he wasn't dreaming and hurried to the house of Mary, the mother of John Mark.

Many people had gathered there to pray—probably for his release. When the servant girl who answered the door heard Peter's voice, she was so startled she ran back inside house without opening the gate.

"It's Peter! It's Peter!" she exclaimed.

"You're crazy," they told her.

But when she kept insisting, they said—and listen to this, "It must be his angel" (Acts 12:15).

You can read right over this little sentence and miss the point. This probably suggests, although the text is not teaching this outright, that the early church believed each person had an accompanying angel who resembled him or her. This passage, more than any other, hints that each of us has a personal guardian angel.

Genesis 48:16 may be another, although the mention of the angel is similarly incidental, not definitive. Jacob prayed,

> The angel who has delivered me from all harm
>   may he bless these boys [the sons of Joseph,
>   Manasseh and Ephraim].

Does everyone have a personal angel? The Bible does not rule out the possibility, but it doesn't come right out and say it either. We do know from Acts 12, however, that an angel supernaturally rescued Peter from a dark prison.

A parallel account is found in Corrie ten Boom's remarkable story of angelic protection at Ravensbruck, the dreadful Nazi prison camp:

> Together we entered the terrifying building. At a table were women who took away all our possessions. Everyone had to undress completely and then go to a room where her hair was checked.
>
>   I asked a woman who was busy checking the possessions of the new arrivals if I might use the toilet. She pointed to a door, and I discovered that the convenience was nothing more than a hole in the shower-room floor. Betsie stayed

close beside me all the time. Suddenly I had an inspiration, "Quick, take off your woolen underwear," I whispered to her. I rolled it up with mine and laid the bundle in a corner with my little Bible. The spot was alive with cockroaches, but I didn't worry about that. I felt wonderfully relieved and happy. "The Lord is busy answering our prayers, Betsie," I whispered. "We shall not have to make the sacrifice of all our clothes."

We hurried back to the row of women waiting to be undressed. A little later, after we had had our showers and put on our shirts and shabby dresses, I hid the roll of underwear and my Bible under my dress; but I prayed, "Lord, *cause now thine angels to surround me*; and let them not be transparent today, for the guards must not see me." I felt perfectly at ease. Calmly I passed the guards. Everyone was checked, from the front, the sides, the back. Not a bulge escaped the eyes of the guard. The woman just in front of me had hidden a woolen vest under her dress; it was taken from her. They let me pass, for they did not see me. Betsie, right behind me, was searched.

But outside awaited another danger. On each side of the door were women who looked everyone over for a second time. They felt over the body of each one who passed. I knew they would not see me, for the angels were still surrounding me. I was not even surprised when they passed me by; but within me rose the jubilant cry, "O Lord, if Thou does so answer prayer, I can face even Ravensbruck unafraid."[17]

WHEN ANGELS "FAIL" US

Angelic protection? Why would angels do little more than help Corrie ten Boom hide her Bible, when in the book of Acts an angel got Peter clean out of prison? This is a secondary lesson we can learn from Acts 12. Angelic intervention, much like the protection of God himself, is not always predictable. And the reasons are not always clear. The angel who personally escorted

Peter from prison failed, if I dare use the term, to prevent the death of James, the brother of John (see Acts 21:1-2). I don't really have an explanation for this imponderable. No one does.

No one has ever fully and adequately answered the question, "Why do bad things happen to good people?" Or its corollary, "Why do angels help people sometimes but not all the time?" Not that people haven't tried to answer the question. The oldest book in the Bible, Job, tries to unravel this unexplainable mystery. I have, too. If God is omni-powerful, and he has legions of angels too, and if God is omni-loving, why do bad things happen to the ones he protects and loves? The purely logical answer is that either God is not all-powerful or he is not all-loving. But this is a far too simplistic conclusion for such a complex issue.

In some ways I believe it has to do with God wanting to preserve our freedom of choice, the essence of our humanity. The potential in human nature for great goodness necessitates the potential—to the same degree—of overwhelming evil. It is an inescapable fact of life as we know it.

But why do guardian angels intervene for some saints like Peter, and not others like James? Why do guardian angels save some children and not others? Why do guardian angels prevent some car accidents and not others? What good is a bodyguard if he doesn't guard your body all the time?

I don't know the whole answer to that question. We *do* know, however, that the kingdom of God is at hand, but it hasn't fully come. We have only *"tasted...* the powers of the coming age," as the anonymous writer of Hebrews explains (Heb 6:5). What God does for us in this life is just an appetizer. We're still waiting for the full meal.

Earlier in his epistle, the writer of Hebrews cites Psalm 8:

What is man that you are mindful of him,
the son of man that you care for him?
You made him a little lower than the angels;
you crowned him with glory and honor
and put everything under his feet.   Hebrews 2:6-8 (italics mine)

The text continues, "In putting everything under him, God left nothing that is not subject to him. *Yet at present* we do not see everything subject to him. *But we see Jesus*" (Heb 2:8-9). It is clear from this Scripture that *at present* not everything is the way we would like it. Not everything is subject to us, even though we are just a little lower than the angels. But we see Jesus. He is the resurrection and the life, the hope of every believer, that somehow, some way, *God's way*, everything is going to work together for good. Not everything that happens to us is good, but God will work it out for good.

This is the tension between what some call the "now" and the "not yet," between "what is" and "what ought to be." For whatever unexplained heavenly reasons, there are many times when God chooses to intervene directly in our lives—*now*. Often God's help is a direct answer to our prayers. Other times, he sustains us even when we don't know what to pray. We only know that it is God answering our prayers, orchestrating our circumstances, ordering our private world, and shaping our destiny.

Other times, more often than we would like, God does not intervene in the "now." For whatever unexplained heavenly reasons, neither he nor his guardian angels steps in to rescue us. Those are the moments when the kingdom of God has *not yet* fully come. We might even start wondering if there is a God. Or if there is, does he care? Maybe God isn't all-loving, we think.

Why would the angel that saved Peter stand at a distance and watch James put to death with the sword? I'm not exactly sure. Sometimes I'm so unsure about these kinds of situations that it makes me angry.

And yet when I think about it, I have to be profoundly grateful for the angel who opened Peter's prison. And for all the angels who have helped and saved numberless saints and sinners through the centuries. Including me.

I like the way the three men in the fiery furnace explained it.

Shadrach, Meshach and Abednego replied to the king, "O Nebuchadnezzar, we do not need to defend ourselves before you in this matter. If we are thrown into the blazing furnace, the God we serve is able to save us from it, and he will rescue us from your hand, O king. *But even if he does not,* we want you to know, O king, that we will not serve your gods or worship the image of gold you have set up."

Daniel 3:16-18 (italics mine)

You know how the account ends, don't you? The king threw them into the flames, an inferno so hot it killed the executioners. But wait! Suddenly Nebuchadnezzar leaped to his feet in amazement. There before his eyes were *four* men *alive* in the furnace! "Look!" the king exclaimed. "I see four men walking around in the fire, unbound and unharmed, and the fourth looks like a son of the gods." It was an angel! A great guardian angel.

God had saved the three men. They knew he could. But if he hadn't, they would have accepted that too. Sometimes God and his angels intervene. Sometimes what God does is obvious and we are profoundly grateful. Other times God and his angels do nothing, or so it appears. But "even if he does not," God is still God and we must still serve him faithfully.

LITTLE CHILDREN AND THEIR ANGELS

Guardian angels are especially necessary for children. If you have raised one or more—we have three—you know how often they hurt themselves. And do irresponsible things. And how helpless we are to protect them.

Could You spare some Guardian Angels
To give me peace of mind
As my children wander from me
And stretch the ties that bind?
Betty Banner[18]

Our daughter was just a few months old. My wife laid her on the waist-high changing table and bent down—for just a fraction of a second—to grab a clean diaper. As she lifted her head, she was horrified to see Shari's little body tumbling to the floor. But was our little girl harmed? Not even slightly. Did my wife see an angel? Nope. But who knows?!

On two occasions a couple years apart, I watched in helpless, frozen fear as each of our first two kids propelled their walkers down a half-flight of stairs. The first time was bad enough, but I really couldn't believe it when I saw the replay. How could I let this happen? Not once, but twice? How did they survive without an injury? Was it their guardian angels? Only God knows.

As supremely important as children are to us, the Bible tells only generally about how God works in their behalf. What happens to children when they die? Should they be baptized? Is there such a thing as an "age of accountability," where children have to make a choice to believe in Christ? Does every child have his or her own personal guardian angel? The Bible just doesn't address these questions as precisely or as thoroughly as do our better theologians.

Jesus did say this, though: "See that you do not look down on one of these little ones. For I tell you that their angels in heaven always see the face of my Father...." Somehow the angels of God take care of our little children, and that's so comforting!

Cheryl Sacks shared the following experience she had with her small daughter:

It was the summer of 1986, and we had just celebrated Nicole's fifth birthday. My husband Hal was away on a trip to the Philippines, and Nicole had been quite anxious about her daddy leaving. So before he left, Hal pulled together our little family of three and prayed for the protection of the Lord over us while he was away. He prayed specifically that God would give his angels charge over us.

One night while Hal was gone, Nicole awoke to the sound of singing. She said that in the night angels came and stood in a circle around her bed and sang the most beautiful songs she had ever heard. I asked her what the angels looked like. "Some were big," she said. "Their heads almost touched the ceiling, and some were little like me." She also told me they were dressed in very bright white and had gold bands around their heads.

Hector Torres shared with me a similar experience with his little daughter. Hector told the story in the previous chapter of the angels in the Jeep who helped him fix his car.

One night, when our daughter Heidy was about five years old, my wife and I were awakened by her screams. We ran to her room, and as we entered, Heidy began pointing to the left side of her bed and said to us, "Look at him, the big white man. Look, look!"

My wife and I couldn't see anything, but Heidy kept insisting there was a big man dressed in white by her bed. I sat by her side and told her that this must have been her guardian angel and that God had allowed her to see him so that she would know how he provided God's children with protection from evil.

In my next account, a friend Dan McGee provides sensitive insights about the ways of God and his angels.

My wife Merrianne and I started praying for our future children three years before our marriage in 1987, and seven years before our first child, Michael, was born. We prayed specifically for God's blessing and anointing on their lives—and that they would know God at a very early age. We believe strongly in the power of prayer and made this a part of our daily supplication, a kind of spiritual investment in our family.

In the first few months of Michael's life, we began noticing something unusual about his behavior. There were times when we would be playing with Michael on a blanket or in his baby carrier, and he would suddenly look past us and begin staring intently up into space, but his eyes would be focused. We would follow his gaze only to see that he was seemingly staring at a blank wall or a meaningless spot on the ceiling.

In those moments, he would smile, and many times he would raise his arms in the air and begin "talking." We also noticed that our presence did not distract his gaze or divert his attention. These occurrences spanned several months.

Lost in the newness of parenthood, we thought little of these episodes until the day my wife commented: "I wonder if he is talking to his angels." It hit us like a revelation.

We would be the last people in the world to try and convince anyone that Michael saw or felt the presence of angelic beings. Yet we believe God has blessed him with a wonderful spiritual awareness as a direct answer to our prayers years before he was born.

ADULTS AND THEIR ANGELS

Adults have wonderful stories to tell of their guardian angels, too.

Definitely an angel. A friend, Anna (not her real name), has done extensive outreach ministry in limited access areas. In 1986 she was working for a large missions organization in central Europe, and I had just seen her a few days before in Vienna when she had the following experience:

Toward the end of May, 1986, about five days after you visited me in Austria, our ministry team had work to do in several cities in Romania. What I am about to share involves two of our team members, Sarah and Claire (not their real names either), whose ministry assignment took them to Bucharest.

They arrived late in the day. Although it was already getting dark in the city, they prayed and agreed that Claire should be the one to walk to the home of a particular Christian believer to arrange a meeting at a later time. Everything had to be done secretly and cautiously because of the terrible persecution of Christians in Romania at that time.

Hearts pounding with fear and excitement, they parked their

vehicle about three quarters of a mile from the home. Sarah waited in the car while Claire headed down the dark street.

About half way to the house, Claire passed a group of about a half a dozen strange men. She knew she was in big trouble when they began to follow her. Picking up her step, she began to pray as she walked as fast as she could toward a dimly lighted intersection just ahead.

Across that intersection, silhouetted in the hazy darkness, stood another man. Something prompted her to approach him. She raced across the street, the other men following her closely and reaching out to grab her.

In English she pleaded with the stranger to please help her. Stepping quickly toward her, he put his arm around her, and, to her stunned amazement, instructed her in perfect English, "Just pretend you're my fiancée and walk with me."

The other men gave up their pursuit, but the stranger stayed by her side. Cautiously she asked him, "Who are you? And what were you doing there at the intersection?"

Again, in perfect English, he answered simply, "My purpose here on earth is to help you."

Not too far away was a hotel. He walked her into the old lobby. Assuring her that she would be safe there, he stepped back outside and vanished into the night. At the stranger's advice, she spent the night at the hotel—much to the distress of her partner who was waiting all this time in their car! But the next day they were reunited, and that evening they were able to complete their assignment.

A stranger on the bus. Patricia Trently tells her angelic encounter:

I'm sixty years old, but I've only been a Christian for the last fifteen years. When I was nineteen, I ran away to New York City with a broken heart. I quit my job, bought a one-way bus ticket, and left Niagara Falls for the big city. I was so emotional, I only took a few personal belongings and twenty dollars. I figured I'd just make it somehow. I'd get a job and I'd be okay.

About fifty miles down the road, I developed a ferocious toothache. Hearing me cry, a young man sitting in the seat in front of me turned around and asked me what was wrong. I told him about my tooth, and he asked if he could sit next to me. I agreed. To my surprise, he pulled a bottle of tooth drops out of his pocket! Not only did the drops take care of the pain, but I found myself opening my heart to him.

When we finally arrived in New York, the stranger told me to wait there in the bus station. He would be right back, he told me. I saw him use a telephone, and when he returned, he passionately entreated me to return to my home. He would even ride back with me, he said, as he held up two return tickets to Niagara.

I could hardly believe it. There I was back on the bus, on my way home after just a few hours in New York City. I was still chattering away at the young man as we got off the bus in Niagara. He was right there behind me, but as I stepped down to the sidewalk and turned around to thank him—he was gone!

I looked frantically up and down the street. I even climbed back on the bus to look for him. He wasn't anywhere to be found! And no one I asked remembered seeing him there with me. He had just vanished.

I never told anyone about this for years. I figured they would think I was crazy! I didn't know what to think! I only knew that I was back home, safe, and I still had my twenty dollars in my pocket!

Twenty-five years later I became a Christian. *Then I knew what had happened to me.* It was God taking care of his little girl. I like to think that the stranger on the bus was my personal guardian angel who had come to help me. Only God knows what evil would have befallen me if I had not returned home.

An angel with borrowed wings. Do you believe in guardian angels? Can you believe this next account? I was having dinner with friends in Salem, Oregon. Jack and Ellene Bowden are wonderful people, having committed their retirement years to full-time Christian ministry. During the meal, I told them I was writing a book about angels. Did they have any stories to tell?

"We don't," Ellene replied after a moment of thought. "But my prayer partner, Nancy, had a really unusual experience. I'm not sure if she would want to share it, though."

Well, she did.

Several years ago, I was accompanying my husband on a free vacation he had won at work. Unfortunately, I was not at all happy about this wonderful opportunity to travel. You see, I was terrified of flying. In fact, I was so overcome by fear before the trip that I would not pack my suitcase until the day we left.

As the plane was lifting off the runway, I managed a quick glance out the window. There near the end of the wing of the plane was an angel! It was about the size of a seven- or eight-year-old child, and as far as I could tell, this angel did not have wings of its own!

He had a face, though, although it was not skinlike. His countenance was crystal white and bright with exuberance and happiness. He looked like he enjoyed flying! I felt such peace about our trip.

The angel remained on the wing for hours. When we began our descent over Florida, I saw the angel go straight up into the sky. Mission accomplished. No one else saw the angel, but no one could ever convince me that what I saw wasn't real.

Sleepless in Indonesia. My last report about guardian angels is from a missionary friend, Fran Love, whose husband Rick is the

United States Director of Frontiers, a large international missions organization. Rick and Fran were church planters in Indonesia for a number of years.

We were new missionaries. Rick was gone on a weekend retreat for Indonesian workers interested in evangelizing their neighbors. I was alone in the house, and very sick with a pregnancy.

God had given my husband a promise that I would be able to carry a child to full term. Back home in America I had miscarried several times and had been unable to carry a pregnancy to term, so I was dreading the loss of this child.

In the middle of the night Rick was gone, something awakened me. I looked toward the foot end of my bed, where I saw the silhouette of a man holding an upraised sword. His dark shape filled the entrance of the open door, and he looked as though he would strike me where I lay.

Honestly, my first feeling was fear. "It's a demon," I thought to myself. Yet the overriding impression was that this was an angel, and that far from trying to harm me, he had been sent to protect me. Indeed, the very stance of the upraised sword showed how clearly I was in danger—and the readiness of the angel to fight for me.

In my heart, I knew with certainty that this was an angel. At that very moment, beautiful praise and worship songs came from my heart and lips. Such peace and joy flooded my body that I quickly fell back into a deep and restful sleep.

I have had two encounters with demonic manifestations, and they were so terrifying that I couldn't sleep without a light in the bedroom. So my ability to sleep so quickly assured me that I had seen an angel.

I also believe it was an angel—and not my imagination—for several reasons. First, I wasn't looking for an appearance, so I wasn't predisposed to this type of supernatural manifestation. In fact, I have never seen an angel before or since.

Second, I felt such peace. Third, the threat of the miscarriage passed.

The fact that the angel was a dark silhouette makes me doubly certain I wasn't imagining things. If I had wanted to conjure up an angel experience, I would have expected to see an image of light, wings, and a halo, more like the angels represented in picture books!

Angels guide us. Angels guard us. Angels carry us into heaven when we die. That's what the next chapter is about.

CHAPTER SIX

Angels on the Edge of Death

With silence only as their bene-
diction
God's angels come
Where, in the shadow of a great
affliction,
The soul sits dumb.
John Greenleaf Whittier

It is quite reasonable to imagine that the unrighteous dead are also carried by God's host to their place of torment. This trip for them, understandably, is no plea-sure ride. **Stephen Swilhart**

W hen my great-grandmother died, as my mother recalls, she heard angels singing. Billy Graham tells almost the same story about his grandmother. When she died, "the room seemed to fill with a heavenly light. She sat up in bed and almost

99

laughingly said, 'I see Jesus. He has His arms outstretched toward me. I see Ben [her husband who had died some years earlier] and I see the angels.'"[1] With that glad exclaim, she took her last breath and passed into eternity.

In that last moment... He will have His angels gather you in their arms to carry you gloriously, wonderfully into heaven.

Billy Graham

WHAT DOES THE BIBLE SAY?

I know you're probably getting tired of hearing me say this, but the Bible is not as specific about this as we would like. Most of what we know from the Bible about angels and death is based on inference corroborated by the experiences of dying people.

Jesus told us a little about this when he shared the story of Lazarus and the rich man.[2] Covered with disgusting sores, the sickly beggar Lazarus was grateful even for garbage that fell from the rich man's table. But when both he and the rich man died, Lazarus went to paradise; the rich man went to hades. At its core, the passage, ultimately, is an indictment of the unbelieving Jewish religious community at the time of Christ, but the incidental reference to angels is important: "The time came," Jesus said, "when the beggar died *and the angels carried him to Abraham's side*" (Lk 16:22, italics mine).

The angels came to transport his spirit into the presence of God. The unusual report in Jude 9 is similar: "Even the archangel Michael, when he was disputing with the devil about the body of Moses, did not dare to bring a slanderous accusation against him." The body of Moses, you might know, vanished after his death. God took him, we are told in the Old Testament, and personally buried him in Moab (Dt 34:5-6). For some reason, which may have had to do with the prophetic reappearance of Moses before the coming of the Lord,[3] there was a heated dispute between Michael and Satan over possession of the body of Moses. We cannot know with certainty why Satan wanted Moses' cadaver, but one thing is clear: angels, dark and light, were hovering around his deathbed.

Angels appear on the edge of death because death is the threshold between time and eternity. Death is a room with a view beyond the veil. In the Bible, nearly every encounter with heaven—visions, dreams, miracles, revelations about the future, the Second Coming of Christ and the Day of Judgment—is enveloped in the presence of angels. If death is the door to eternity, angels are the doormen. They were, in fact, the gatekeepers at the empty tomb of the Savior! Angels were all around, witnessing the resurrection and announcing it to his disciples.

Another Bible narrative that connects angels and death is 2 Kings 2, the famous account of Elijah speeding to heaven in a fiery chariot. Elisha had received a premonition about his mentor Elijah's departure, and as the two men were walking along and talking together, "suddenly a chariot of fire and horses of fire appeared and separated the two of them, and Elijah went up to heaven in a whirlwind. When Elisha saw this, he cried out, 'My father! My father! The chariots and horsemen of Israel!' And Elisha saw him no more" (2 Kgs 2:12).

This passage says nothing directly about angels, but there is a good chance that "the chariots and horsemen of Israel" is a veiled reference to angelic hosts for at least two reasons. First, just a few pages later, in 2 Kings 6:17, when Elisha is trapped in the city of Dothan, he and his servant saw the hills around the city "full of horses and chariots of fire." Angels! Second, the chariots of fire are similar to Ezekiel's vision of the cherubim in the first chapter of his book. By deduction, then, angels were probably in the whirlwind that blew Elijah into heaven.

Catholic angelologist Pascal Parente writes, "It is at the hour of death that the good angel shows the greatest zeal in protecting and defending the soul committed to his care, invoking often the assistance of other angels against the wiles and fury of Satan." He adds that, according to Origen, "At the hour of death the celestial escort [*psychopompe* in Greek] receives the soul the moment before it leaves the body."[4]

HOW NEAR-DEATH EXPERIENCES CORROBORATE
WHAT THE BIBLE SAYS

George Gallup, of all people (actually he is a Christian!), reported a wonderful near-death experience (NDE) in his book *Adventures in Immortality*. A nurse, who lives in Pennsylvania, became deathly ill after the birth of her first child. A voice told her she was going to die, so she called her husband and other members of the family into her room to tell them. At that moment, she recounted, she fell into a trance and had a vision.

> It seemed that all these angels came from heaven and, holding hands, they formed a stairway reaching all the way up to heaven... I kept going up this stair of angels' hands until I reached heaven. When I reached the top, there was a great mist before the door, and an angel said to me, "That mist is your family's prayers for your return."[5]

Modern trauma care and life-saving technology have dramatically increased the number of people who have had NDEs—a medical phenomenon whereby a patient has the sense of leaving his or her body due to some crisis such as accident or illness. This experience is frequently accompanied by a temporary cessation of vital body functions like respiration and pulse, until the patient regains consciousness a short time later. According to a recent article in *Life* magazine, pollsters have estimated that some eight million Americans have had NDEs.

The apostle Paul survived an NDE and wrote about his experience in 2 Corinthians 12:2-4. We think it may have happened when he was stoned—almost to death—in Lystra (see Acts 14:19). Paul reported,

> I know a man in Christ [a veiled reference to himself] who fourteen years ago was caught up to the third heaven [paradise, the realm of God in ancient cosmology]. Whether it was in the body or out of the body I do not know—God

knows. And I know that this man—whether in the body or apart from the body I do not know, but God knows—was caught up to paradise. He heard inexpressible things, things that man is not permitted to tell.

We wish Paul would have mentioned the angels, but he does let us know, *in God's Word*, that it is possible to have an "out of body experience," to be caught up into heaven and to live to tell about it.

I should probably point out, because of all the current rage about out of body experiences, that Paul's experience was not self-induced by mind-bending meditation, which is encouraged by adherents of the New Age movement. For Paul, it just happened, and it probably happened because he was dying.

Paul gives us no details about what he saw, but the careful study of NDEs has uncovered many common denominators. People who have been on the brink of death, it seems, have very similar stories to tell.

Raymond Moody, M.D., author of *Life after Life* (over seven million copies sold!) observes,

Despite the wide variation in the circumstances surrounding close calls with death and in the types of persons undergoing them, it remains true that there is a striking similarity among the accounts of the experiences themselves. In fact, the similarities among various reports are so great that one can easily pick out about fifteen separate elements which recur again and again in the mass of narratives I have collected.[6]

This is especially significant in that much of the current research has been with people who have not read about NDEs or talked with others who had had similar experiences. Indeed, many of the people interviewed for books like *Life after Life* thought their own experiences were unique.

The problem with many NDEs, as real as they may seem, is that they are not strictly biblical. A glaring example is a best-selling book, *Embraced by the Light*, where the writer's experience in heaven challenges many basic Christian teachings, like the nature and identity of Christ. The Bible must be our point of reference for understanding and judging NDEs, not the other way around. If we start using NDEs to understand the Bible, we'll be lost in an anything-goes theology, because NDEs can be as misleading as they are enchanting.

Corrado Balducci, a theologian whose specializes in demonology and the paranormal, was quoted recently, "These 'postmortem visions' can be looked upon as good, but we can't go beyond that. They cannot be considered proof of the hereafter because proof of the hereafter comes to us only from the Word of God... God wants faith from us. If someone believes in an afterlife simply because he had such an experience, he is making a big mistake."[7] If NDEs point us to Jesus, great! If they lull us into a contrived peace about death and dying, they are a terrible deception.

My point in bringing up the subject, however, is that NDE research *generally*, in the broadest sense, authenticates the teaching of the Bible on death and heaven, in that nearly every NDE includes the appearance of a being or beings of light. God. Jesus. Angels. In the case where an NDE contradicts what we know through Scripture, however, such any being may be a dark angel disguised as an angel of light.

Children and NDEs. Most remarkable are the NDEs of little children. Diane Komp, an oncologist and professor of pediatrics at Yale University, did not start out her adult life as a believer. "When I was in medical school," she told *Life* magazine, "I was hanging out somewhere on that nebulous continuum between agnostic and atheist." Her encounters with terminally ill children, according to the *Life* article, "changed all that. She now writes in an openly Christian manner about using what she has learned to help dying children and their families prepare for death."[8]

Early in her medical career, Komp sat with the family of a

child in the last stages of leukemia. Komp recounts the moment of the child's death: "She had the final energy to sit up and say, 'The angels—they're so beautiful! Mommy, can you see them? Do you hear their singing? I've never heard such beautiful singing.'"[9] Angels were carrying her little soul into the presence of God!

WHEN LOVED ONES DIE:
ANGELS OF PROTECTION AND COMFORT

Sometimes people see angels when they are near death. Other times, angels bring a sense of comfort to those who are left behind. A member of our church, Mike Lambly, wrote to me about his experience with his little daughter Katherine, born several months early.

Katherine was born weighing all of one pound, nine ounces and was quickly rushed off to the neonatal unit. She looked perfect—every little finger and toe was there, just in miniature. We were so happy she was alive. And there was hope—hope for a miracle.

The cards and flowers and congratulations came, the loving letters and notes of encouragement and prayer. And every day Katherine lived was a miracle. Three days. Then five. Then seven. The doctors were amazed!

A week after her birth, I decided to go see Katherine during the day between my sales calls. As I walked the hospital halls to the neonatal unit, I thought of my tiny baby and the long fight that was ahead of her. I reached the special care unit and pulled on the required gown. Pushing up my sleeves to perform the obligatory fingers-to-elbow scrubbing, I turned to look through the large glass window to see Katherine lying in her incubator and glanced around at some of the other babies.

I looked back towards Katherine as I kept scrubbing. Suddenly I stopped motionless over the basin, transfixed at the sight of two very large figures standing on either side of her incubator. They had to be at least ten feet tall, with very large shoulders. And they shined with the brightest white light I have ever seen. I could see no face to determine if the beings were male or female, but as I stared, I knew they were angels and I was certain they were there to protect my daughter. The length of their appearance was very brief, and yet it seemed as if time stood still forever.

I walked over to the incubator and saw Katherine lying there peacefully with her little cap on to keep her warm. I told her that all would be well and that not only did Jesus love her, but that she had angels watching over her and protecting her. I couldn't wait to share the news with my wife Jeanne that the Lord had sent angels to watch over and protect our baby. And that everything was going to be fine.

But by the next day, Katherine was gone. We had a wonderfully peaceful memorial service, but in the days that followed, I began to question the Lord: "Why did you send those angels? I thought they were there to protect my daughter, to keep her safe as she grew."

I'm sure it was no coincidence that Jeanne and I just happened to watch Billy Graham on television about two weeks later. His subject: angels. The believer, he declared, is never out of the Lord's care. Even at our death, he provides angels to usher us into his presence. Yes, the angels that visited Katherine's incubator had a mission, but it was not just to protect her. More importantly, they came to take her to Jesus.

The angels came for her husband. A friend of a friend, Sylvia Wentworth, sent me this wonderful story about an angelic visitation and the death of her husband:

My husband had not been feeling well for some time. One evening, late in 1974, he went to bed quite early while I stayed up well past midnight. It may have been as late as 1 A.M. when I finally joined him. As I quietly slipped under the covers, I turned over toward my husband. His back was facing me.

Right there, on my husband's side of the bed was this figure, this huge figure of a man standing there, looking at my husband. He was maybe seven or eight feet tall. I'm not really sure. I just know he was a huge being, but not fat! He had his hands clasped over his heart, and I can remember how he was looking down on my sleeping husband. He never looked in my direction.

I was especially moved by the intense compassion in his eyes. The angel reminded me of a young mother looking into the face of her first newborn child. There was such love! It was like nothing I'd ever seen or felt.

Though I know he was large, I can't really say what he was wearing, but it wasn't a suit. It was something loose, like a robe. I'm not sure if it was white either, or perhaps a kind of tan. One thing about him I remember, though, is that I could almost see through him.

The reason I'm unsure about these details was his eyes. The only thing I can really remember is his loving eyes.

All this happened in just a few seconds. I blinked my eyes and he was gone. But I knew then, at that moment, that my husband would not be with me much longer. Indeed, a couple of months later on a Friday evening, my husband fell into a coma. A few days later he slipped away to be with the Lord. I was so at peace, because I had the knowledge deep in my heart, from the angel appearance, that my husband would be in heaven soon.

Comforting angels of all kinds. Another acquaintance of mine, Kelli, saw an angel in a dream, but the dream was as real to Kelli as the bedside angel in Sylvia's encounter.

When I became a Christian, late in 1990, I found myself especially burdened for my aging grandfather. Several strokes had left him bedridden in a nursing home. He couldn't speak.

In spite of his disabilities, I decide to tell him about Jesus and how he had changed my life. Explaining to him how Jesus was in my heart, I asked him if he had a relationship with God. His eyes were closed.

"If Jesus is in your heart, grandpa, open your eyes and look at me." He did! And his eyes filled with tears! I cried too, because I was so happy.

A few weeks later, the very night before he died, I had a dream about a huge angel with golden blond hair—and wings spread out across the sky. My family and I were crossing the ocean on a large ship when a voice announced that someone had died. It was my grandfather.

At that moment I looked up at the angel covering the sky above. He was holding back the powers of darkness, shielding us below. Nothing could get by him! Looking watchfully, first to the left, then to the right, he turned toward me and said, "Don't be afraid. Your grandfather is going to be with the Lord." The angel spoke with such a calm, gentle voice, and I felt such peace in his presence.

The very next day my grandfather died.

A close friend, Susan Hunt, told me of an equally powerful experience at the death of her grandmother just a year ago.

My grandmother was in the hospital less than a week before she died. I flew in to be there to see her, and she was alert and lucid to the end. She recited the 23rd Psalm (her favorite Scripture) with the family and her pastor. All of us were gathered around her bed for the last hours of her life. It was so moving and beautiful.

Because there were so many family members present, we had to take turns visiting with her. I had two turns. During each of those brief visits, as I sat on the windowsill by her bed, I noticed something out of the corner of my eye. At the time I dismissed it because I thought my tears were somehow distorting the light in the room. But I can remember distinctly seeing a bright, white—almost blue-white—"light" with a gentle waving motion, as if a soft breeze were blowing a sheer curtain. I remember thinking at the time how strange it was that I would see the same thing in the same place, twice. But when I turned my head to look at it directly, the aura vanished.

My grandmother died that day.

A couple of months later, my mother's youngest sister asked me if I had see the angel in Grandma's hospital room the afternoon she died. I had not told anyone what I had seen. And neither had my aunt. I asked her, "Was it in the corner of the room next to the head of her bed?"

"Yes!" she exclaimed. In fact, she had seen the evidence of the angel off and on for a couple hours.

I described in detail what I had seen and asked her if it matched what she saw.

"Yes!" she replied. She also mentioned, before I had said anything about it, that when she looked directly at the bluish light, it would vanish.

REFLECTIONS ON OUR GREATEST LIGHT, JESUS

Only a small minority have had NDEs. Even then, coming *near* death is only a temporary reprieve. Sooner or later, we must all die and reach our final destination—whether that be heaven or hell.

But near-death experiences are real. Even reputable medical researchers have acknowledged this, although there are some studies that suggest NDEs can be explained physiologically. Regardless, unusual things sometimes happen to people at the moment of death. They see beings of light; sometimes they see deceased friends and family members. But NDEs tell us nothing about who God is and what he expects of us. At best, NDEs are clinical-religious experiences which hint at life after death.

Only God's Word can give us any certain ideas about life and death, heaven and hell, and yet reading about angels and near-death experiences has to make you think. About God. About yourself.

The greatest "proof" of life after death is not the angels. It is the resurrection of Jesus from the dead. The apostle Paul, a highly educated man and once the principal opponent of Christianity, met Jesus personally. It changed his life. It changed history, too.

Paul wrote of Christ, "that he was buried, that he was raised on the third day... he appeared to Peter, and then to the Twelve. After that, he appeared to more than five hundred of the brothers at the same time, most of whom are still living... Then he appeared to James, then to all the apostles, and last of all he appeared to me also" (1 Cor 15:3-8). The resurrected Christ is the cornerstone of Christianity.

My confidence is not in angels, as grateful as I am for their invisible intervention in my life, and for all the accounts I've told you so far in this book. And my salvation is not mediated by angels. Beyond the name of Jesus, there is no other name given among men by which we can be saved (Acts 4:12).

Knowing that angels will carry us from our bed of death to the bosom of Abraham, to the front step of heaven, is of little consequence in the brighter light of the glorious resurrection of Christ. That's why Paul could write so confidently, "Death has been swallowed up in victory. Where, O death, is your victory? Where, O death, is your sting?" (1 Cor 15:54-55). Without Jesus, there would be no resurrection. Without Jesus, there would be no hope. Without Jesus, there would be no angels.

"He is the image of the invisible God, the firstborn over all creation. For by him all things were created: things in heaven and on earth, visible and invisible, whether thrones or powers or rulers or authorities" (Col 1:15-16). Or angels.

CHAPTER SEVEN

Angels in Disguise

Do not forget to entertain strangers, for by so doing some people have entertained angels without knowing it. **Hebrews 13:2**

Undercover angels posing as humans? The idea is a little unnerving. I mean, I meet strangers all the time—and sometimes I'm not very polite to them!

"Angels unawares" is God's way of keeping us guessing. It's proof that God doesn't want us to know everything, to understand everything, to explain everything. Coincidence, someone once said, is God performing a miracle anonymously.

ABRAHAM AND LOT

Angels in disguise appear again and again in the Bible, especially in the Old Testament. One of the more notable examples is recorded in Genesis 18 and 19, the account of Abraham and the prophetic announcement of Isaac's birth followed by the account of Lot and the destruction of Sodom and Gomorrah.

The narrative begins with three "men" appearing to Abraham near the great trees of Mamre. "Abraham looked up and saw three men standing nearby. When he saw them, he hurried from the entrance of his tent to meet them" (Gn 18:2).

In the spirit of Semitic protocol, Abraham bowed before his guests and offered them a meal. "Let me get you something to eat," he said.

So Abraham hurried into his tent to Sarah, his elderly wife. "Quick," he said, "get several quarts of fine flour and bake some bread." Then he ran to the herd and selected a choice, tender calf and gave it to a servant who rushed to prepare it. As Abraham set the bread and veal before them, his guests actually ate the food.

What a disguise! Not only did the angels appear human, but they even had lunch with Abraham! But they had not come just to share a friendly meal. A couple of messages were burning in their spirits.

The first message was about Abraham's miracle son, Isaac. The angels announced that Abraham and his wife Sarah, who was way past child-bearing age, were going to have a son! Sarah laughed scornfully in disbelief when she overheard the prediction, but God always gets the last laugh. About a year later, when the miracle boy was born, Abraham gave him the name Isaac, which means "laughter." Sarah said, "God has brought me laughter, and everyone who hears about this will laugh with me" (Gn 21:1-7).

The *second message* seemed like an afterthought. As the angels were about to leave, they looked toward Sodom, and the Lord said to himself, "Shall I hide from Abraham what I am about to do?... The outcry against Sodom and Gomorrah is so great and their sin so grievous that I will go down and see if what they have done is as bad as what I have heard."

The two messengers (we are not told what happened to the third individual) arrived at Sodom in the evening, probably the same day they had visited Abraham. When Lot saw them, he bowed down like Abraham had done and insisted they stay in his home. But before Lot and his family had gone to bed, all the men from every part of the city surrounded Lot's house. They hollered at Lot, "Where are those men who came to you tonight? Bring them out to us so that we can have sex with them!" How disgusting! Little did the Sodomites outside know they were clamoring for angels.

Lot tried to reason with the townsfolk, to no avail, and the mysterious messengers came to his rescue. "The men inside"— the Bible is still calling them *men*—"reached out and pulled Lot back into the house and shut the door. Then they struck the men who were at the door with blindness so that they could not find the door." Now we know they were angels!

"With the coming of dawn," the Bible narrative continues, "the angels urged Lot, saying, 'Hurry! Take your wife and your two daughters who are here, or you will be swept away when the city is punished" (Gn 19:15).

I've left a lot of details out of the narration in order to draw your attention to one thing: messenger angels appeared in human form, yet the boundary between their angel nature and their human forms is not clear. Other than the honor given them by Abraham and Lot, and their special burst of blinding power in Sodom, we can hardly tell if these "men" are, in fact, angels. This Old Testament narrative exemplifies the mystery of angels and the enigma of the spiritual dimension, something I discussed at length in the first chapter. The boundary between earth and heaven is unclear.

Furthermore, there's even a suggestion in the text that one of the angels was Yahweh himself. In the tenth verse of the chapter we read, "*Then the Lord said*, 'I will surely return to you about this time next year, and Sarah your wife will have a son." This is undoubtedly a veiled reference to "the Angel of the Lord," someone we will examine more closely in the next chapter.

MANOAH AND HIS WIFE

A similar account appears in Judges 13, the story of the birth of Samson. "A certain man of Zorah, named Manoah, from the clan of the Danites, had a wife who was sterile and remained childless. The angel of the Lord appeared to her and said, 'You are going to conceive and have a son. No razor may be used on his head'"(Jgs 13:2-5). This is the beginning of the infamous story of Samson and his long hair.

"Then the woman went to her husband and told him, 'A man of God came to me.'" She added—and notice these words, "'*He looked like an angel of God, very awesome.* I didn't ask him where he came from, and he didn't tell me his name'" (Jgs 13:6).

Did Manoah have a little bit of a hard time believing his wife's story? We're not told, but he prayed to the Lord for the angel to return, to teach him how to bring up this special boy. God heard his prayer, and the angel reappeared, but—oddly—not to Manoah. "The angel of God came again to the woman while she was out in the field; but her husband Manoah was not there with her" (Jgs 13:9). She had to run back to the house to let her husband know the angel had returned! And the angel just waited there in the field!

"He's here! The man [she doesn't call him an angel] who appeared to me the other day!"

So Manoah got up and followed his wife back into the field. There he was. The man. The angel. Waiting to talk. "Are you the same man who talked to my wife the other day?"

"Yes," the angel replied.

So Manoah asked him a few things about his son to be. He also asked him to stay for a meal.

The angel of the Lord replied, "Even though you detain me,

I will not eat any of your food." Remember, he did eat with Abraham! "But if you prepare a burnt offering, offer it to the Lord." At this point, the writer adds the little note, in parentheses in the English Bible, "Manoah did not realize it was the angel of the Lord."

So Manoah asked him, "What's your name?"

The angel of the Lord replied gravely, "Why do you ask my name? It is beyond understanding."

Whoa! I would love to know what Manoah was feeling at that moment! At the angel's suggestion, and without asking any more questions, Manoah took a young goat, together with a grain offering, and sacrificed it on a rock to Yahweh. While Manoah and his wife watched, the Bible tells us, the angel of the Lord ascended into heaven on the flames of the barbecue!

Whoa again! "Seeing this, Manoah and his wife fell with their faces to the ground. When the angel of the Lord did not show himself again to Manoah and his wife, Manoah realized that is was the angel of the Lord."

"We are doomed to die!" he said to his wife. "We have seen God!"

But his wife, in a more reasonable frame of mind, reminded him that if God had meant to kill them, they would not be around discussing the angel rocketing to heaven in the smoke of the burnt offering.

"I guess you're right," Manoah admitted sheepishly.

And the woman gave birth to a boy and named him Samson.

You probably realize that I embellished this story a bit, and I'm hoping I haven't offended you. My purpose is for you to see the mystery in the appearance of angels—and the humor in our ignorance and helplessness to understand fully what's going on.

As a writer for *Guideposts* observed recently, "It's not hard to see why everyone loves a good mystery. And why not? Life itself is mysterious, a matter of awe. Faith in God is a mystery, a matter of wonder and reverence and of trust in things unseen."[1]

In the account of the parents of Samson, the angel—the angel of the Lord it turns out—was so well disguised that

Manoah and his wife weren't sure if it was man or angel. Not only is there sometimes a fine line between angels and men, sometimes there is a fine line between angels and God. Was it a man? Was it an angel? Was it God himself? We may never know. And in one sense it doesn't really matter. What matters is the message, the moment. That God has spoken. Our lives are changed forever and he gets all the credit and glory.

Angels in disguise, or "angels unawares," have what theologians call "assumed bodies." Angels masquerading as human beings are like holographic anthropomorphisms. As we discussed in Chapter 1, human language is simply not adequate to describe God and angels. So to help us, God has portrayed himself—and angels—in the Bible as having certain human qualities that are not meant to be interpreted in a strictly literal sense.

In Psalm 11:4, for example, we are told that the Lord "observes the sons of men; *his eyes* examine them" (italics mine). And in Psalm 89:13, the writer tells God, "*Your arm* is endued with power; *your hand* is strong, *your right hand* exalted." This does not mean that God has eyes, arms and hands; language is being employed to describe God in ways that we can understand. These are called "anthropomorphisms."

One theological dictionary says that anthropomorphisms "designate the view which conceives of God as having *human form*... [and] in a wider sense... *human attributes* and *emotions*." In a similar way, angels take on human form, not only so we can see them, but because in their pure heavenly form, they are so blindingly powerful that we would never get past the power of the moment to hear the message of the day. Angels masquerading as human beings are like holographic anthropomorphisms.

TRUE STORIES OF "ANGELS UNAWARES"

A stranger in the mountains. Carol Akimoff, whose husband is the director of Youth With A Mission (YWAM) Slavic Ministries, wrote to me about her experience:

This story took place in the summer of 1966. Wedge and Shirley Alman were leaders of our YWAM Summer of Service team. In a caravan of several vehicles, we were traversing a rugged, mountainous region of Central America. It also happened to be the worst time of the year—the tropical rainy season.

We were headed for a two month mission outreach among the small villages of the area. We hoped to minister in some of the local prisons as well.

Since early morning we had inched our way over the precarious mountain road. It was the rainy season, and numerous times during the day we had piled out of the cars, vans and camper to apply our combined strength to pushing and praying them out of the over-the-ankle-deep mud. How many times had we been stuck that day? And how many sandals and thongs had been sucked off our feet and disappeared into the oblivion of the mire? We had lost track.

Night found us exhausted and still urging our vehicles forward–up, up and over the mountain. To spend the night there would be unthinkable, at least to these rookie North American missionaries. The darkness was intense. Would the rain never stop? Water and rocks crashed down the side of the mountain. We wondered if they would stop rolling before hitting us. The signs posted along the road warning us to beware of avalanches in the area were certainly no comfort.

Suddenly one vehicle after another chugged to a complete stop. The road had disappeared and in its place we faced the whole side of the mountain that had eroded away from somewhere up over us.

An exploratory trip in our jeep revealed no possible way to negotiate the avalanche. To go forward was impossible until the road equipment arrived the next day to open a way for us.

Wedge asked us all to get out and after several minutes of intense prayer we crawled back into our assigned cars and made ourselves as comfortable as one can get sleeping upright, believing that tomorrow would bring more hope.

Another night in the "YWAM Hilton!" We shivered as we rolled up the windows and locked the doors. Sheer exhaustion would lull us to sleep tonight. The minutes passed.

Suddenly a sharp rap on the window startled us. A man wrapped in a blanket was motioning to Shirley: she cracked the window trembling. Wedge was in another car with some of the guys and our vehicle was full of girls.

He was very excited and was speaking Spanish. Gesturing with his hands, he urged us to move our vehicles to another spot immediately. If we stayed here, we were in great danger. Maneuvering our cars to the spot he had indicated, we took comfort in the fact that the kind man had led us to safety.

When we turned to thank him, he had disappeared as mysteriously as he had appeared.

No one got much sleep the rest of the night. The rocks never stopped rolling down the mountain and the water continued to gush. With sound effects like these, who can sleep!

From what we could tell of the area, there was no place for him to have gone. In fact, there was no place where he could have come from! No vehicle. No house or homestead. Nothing! "That guy must have been an angel!" we agreed.

The next morning, in the hazy light of the new day, we had a grand view of our location—and our predicament. We were perched high on a mountain ridge, a deep canyon on one side, a steep mountain slope on the other.

And on the road just ahead of us, where we had stopped to pray the night before, was a huge landslide, caused no doubt by the heavy rains. Half the mountain ahead of us was parked on the very spot where we had paused less than ten hours earlier!

Now we were sure we had seen an angel!

"Maybe an angel." A member of our church, Anna, has shared with me several accounts of angelic aid; one of which I introduced in Chapter 5, about her experiences in Romania. She titled these experiences "Maybe an angel," because these "good Samaritans" may have been angels in disguise!

I had at least two remarkable experiences. At the time they struck me simply as amazing, and I have yet to decide if they were angels.

The first occurred in Warsaw, Poland, in February of 1986. I happened to be there with some other people on a ministry-related visit. We were also there shopping for our ministry organization based in Austria, because prices were so much lower in Eastern Europe at the time.

At any rate, we were specifically trying to purchase a drafting board so one of our team members could begin publishing an improved newsletter. We found exactly what we were looking for, but for whatever reason the store manager simply refused to sell it to us. He said it was for display only, and couldn't be sold—a common practice in communist countries.

We were about to leave the store empty-handed, when my eye caught a man glancing at us from outside the store. Walking into the store, he spoke to the manager for a couple seconds. A few minutes later we walked out with our drawing board, neatly packed and wrapped.

I realize that this may seem like such an insignificant thing, but having done extensive ministry work under very tense situations in communist nations, every little bit of special provision from the Lord is unforgettable.

The second incident occurred the following year in the spring. I was in Bulgaria with another young woman, one of my ministry partners. We had been driving for some time toward the city of Varna on the Black Sea, and the fuel gauge was inching toward empty. It was getting dark.

There were not very many service stations on the backroads of communist Bulgaria! The very few that did exist were open irregular hours—and not usually towards the end of the day. Getting more anxious by the minute, we finally spotted a gas station. It was open!

But when I pulled in, the woman who was operating the business refused to sell me any gasoline, because I had vouchers for 96 octane and she only had 93 octane. The bureaucracy in Bulgaria was so smothering that even my offer of the more valuable vouchers for cheaper fuel would not penetrate the iron curtain of her mind.

I had given up hope when a black sedan drove into the station behind us. I was surprised when he did not pull up alongside the pumps. Instead, getting out of his car, he walked up to me and asked, in perfect English, "Can I help you?" Remember, I was in a communist state where, because of debilitating fear, help from strangers is virtually non-existent.

Anyway, I explained that I had the wrong octane vouchers and the station operator would not sell me any gas. The stranger turned to the attendant, spoke to her for a couple moments in Bulgarian, and left. Without another objection, the woman proceeded to sell me as much gas as I needed. And we were on our way!

Have you ever considered that, just perhaps, the reason you have gotten as far as you have is because of the invisible work of anonymous angels? Good strangers in the night? I heard a preacher say one time, "The more you believe in coincidences, the more coincidences seem to happen." What happened in your life today, or in the last couple of days, that cannot be explained without talking about God or his angels? As Helen Steiner Rice observed, "On life's busy thoroughfare, we meet with angels unaware."

CHAPTER EIGHT

Archangels, Beasts, and UFOs

As for their rings, they were so high that they were dreadful; and their rings were full of eyes round about them four. And when the living creatures went, the wheels went by them: and when the living creatures were lifted from the earth, the wheels were lifted up.

Ezekiel 1:18-19 (KJV)

Strange and unusual angels. The Bible is full of them. In fact, the Bible describes angels differently than we typically imagine them. In the Old Testament, for example, a good portion of the angel passages are about "the angel of the Lord."

THE ANGEL OF THE LORD

Who was this mysterious visitor who appeared so frequently to men and women in ancient Israel? One of the more notable narratives is recorded in Exodus 3, in the story of the burning bush.

Moses was minding the flock of his father-in-law, Jethro. He was also minding his own business. He probably wasn't looking for angels as he led the sheep to the far side of the desert, to Horeb, the mountain of God.

Suddenly, in a most curious event, "*the angel of the Lord* appeared to him in flames of fire from within a bush. Moses saw that even though the bush was on fire it did not burn up" (Ex 3:2, italics mine). So he did what most of us would do. He said to himself, "I'm going to check this out—why isn't the bush burning up?" (Ex 3:3, paraphrased).

The account, of course, is about how God called Moses to be the great deliverer of the Jewish people, the one who would lead them out of the oppression of Egyptian slavery. It is also, secondarily, about how God speaks to us in unusual ways. In this case, God revealed himself through "the angel of the Lord," the messenger of Yahweh, the *mal'akh Yahweh* in Hebrew.

Who was this being? Was he God himself? If so, why does the Bible call him an angel? But if he was just an angel, why does the Bible seem to present the "angel of Yahweh" as Yahweh himself? In Exodus 3:4, for example, "When the Lord [Yahweh] saw that he [Moses] had gone over to look, *God* called to him from within the bush, 'Moses, Moses.'"

I suppose this could be explained simply by the fact that angels are just so close to God—and represent him so directly and precisely—that it's easy to confuse the angel of the Lord with God himself. In other words, the angel of the Lord really was an angel. This was the view of the ancient Jews, who referred to the angel of the Lord as "the angel of the countenance" and "the highest revelation of the unseen God." A statement from the Talmud, the very old Jewish book of religion, declared that "the Angel of the Lord is united with the most high God by oneness of nature."[1]

Following this Jewish tradition, Catholics for the most part regard the angel of the Lord as a *representative* of God, an actual angel. Protestants, on the other hand, generally believe that the angel of the Lord was either a manifestation of Yahweh himself, or the Messiah making visible appearances centuries before his incarnation, hence the "pre-incarnate Christ." John Calvin wrote, "I am inclined to agree with the ancient writers [the biblical authors], that in those passages wherein it is stated that the angel of the Lord appeared to Abraham, Jacob, and Moses, *Christ was that angel.*"[2]

I concur with Calvin. I believe the angel of the Lord was Jesus in pre-incarnate form. Now the Old Testament does not tell us this directly, but Zechariah 3 comes real close. In a vision, Zechariah the prophet saw Joshua the high priest (not the earlier Joshua of Jericho fame) standing before the angel of the Lord, presumably in heaven. Joshua was dressed in filthy garments, symbolic of Israel's sinful past.

Zechariah was written after the Jewish exile in Babylon, which everyone knew had been the terrible consequence of Israel's idolatry and sin against Yahweh. So Joshua's dirty clothing represented all of the worst of Israel's past. God's prodigal children really had no right to stand in his holy presence. And Satan knew this. He was standing right there to accuse Joshua—and all of the Jewish people he embodied. But the angel of the Lord said to those who were close by, "Take off his filthy clothes." Then, turning to Joshua, he said, "See, I have taken away your sin, and I will put rich garments on you" (Zec 3:4).

This passage perfectly describes the work of Christ, who took upon himself our degradation and shame and, in an inconceivable exchange, covers us with the robes of his righteousness. He is our intermediary, our advocate, our defense attorney who stands between the accusations of Satan and the judgment of the Father. The apostle John wrote, "If anybody does sin, we have one who speaks to the Father in our defense—Jesus Christ the Righteous One" (1 Jn 2:1).

Thus, based on everything we know from the New Testament about the work and ministry of the Lord Jesus, it is very easy to make the connection between the angel of the Lord in Zechariah 3 and the Messiah, the Lamb of God who takes away the sins of the world. The angel of the Lord in the Old Testament is, I believe, the Lord Jesus Christ himself appearing in pre-incarnate form.

HIGHLIGHTS OF THE HEAVENLY HOST

If, indeed, the angel of the Lord is God himself, then he is plainly at the very top of the heavenly hierarchy. He is the Most High. Somewhere down the scale, a distant second, are the archangels.

If the archangel now, perilous, from behind the stars took
even one step down toward us, our own heart,
beating higher and higher, would beat us to death.
Rainer Maria Rilke

Archangels. "Archangel" comes from a compound Greek term *archangelos*—it even looks like the English word—and means "ruling angel." This is actually a very rare word in the Bible, occurring only twice in the New Testament and not at all in the Old. In the first of these two references, it is the voice of the archangel who signals the resurrection of the righteous dead: "For the Lord himself will come down from heaven with a loud command, *with the voice of the archangel* and with the trumpet call of God, and the dead in Christ will rise first" (1 Thes 4:16, italics mine).

The English version reads "*the* archangel," which sounds like there's only one, but that's not quite so clear in the original Greek of the New Testament. If there is a heavenly hierarchy, if there are ranks of authority among the angels, then it is reasonable for us to believe that there may be many archangels, many "ruling angels."

Two archangels are named in the Bible. One is Michael, whose name means "who is like God?" Jude tells us that "the archangel Michael" disputed with the devil about the body of Moses (Jude 9). This is the only other place where the actual word "archangel" appears in Scripture, but Michael is mentioned by name at least ten other times.[3] As we have already seen, Michael served as prince or guardian over the destiny of the Jewish people (see Dn 10:13, 21), and the Book of Revelation speaks of "Michael and his angels" who battled with Satan when the devil rebelled against God in the mists of pre-time (Rv 12:7).

The only other angel in the Bible with a name is Gabriel, which in Hebrew means "one who is as God," or maybe "God is great," or maybe "man of God." Scholars disagree about the precise meaning of his name. We do know, however, that Gabriel appeared to Daniel twice (Dn 8:16; 9:21), both times to interpret prophetic visions, and later in the New Testament to Zacharias, heralding the birth of John the Baptist (Lk 1:19).

Gabriel is never called an archangel in the Bible, but we may assume he is a "ruling angel," because of his crucial task of revealing the redemptive plans of God. All his appearances in the Bible are linked with promises about the coming of the Messiah, his finest hour being his visit with the Virgin Mary, when he announced to her that she would give birth to the Savior (Lk 1:26-28). Oh, what a message! If angels can cry, Gabriel must have wept over that assignment!

Cherubim and Seraphim falling down before Thee
Which, wert and art, and ever more shall be.
Reginald Heber

Seraphim. Little is known of these creatures, as they appear only once in the Bible—in Isaiah 6:

I saw the Lord seated on a throne, high and exalted, and the train of his robe filled the temple. Above him were *seraphs*, each with six wings: With two wings they covered their faces, with two they covered their feet, and with two they were flying. And they were calling to one another:

Holy, holy, holy is the Lord Almighty;
the whole earth is full of his glory. Isaiah 6:1-3

A little later, one of the seraphs soared toward Isaiah. Taking a live coal from the heavenly altar and placing it on Isaiah's mouth (ouch!), the angel declared, "See, this has touched your lips; your guilt is taken away and your sin is atoned for" (Is 6:7).

What you have just read is just about everything we know of the seraphs, or seraphim. Some think this term comes from a Hebrew word meaning "fire" or "burning," but Old Testament scholars are not entirely sure.

Gesenius, one of the most widely respected Hebrew specialists, thought it might be related to an Arabic term, *sarupha*, which means "to be noble." He thought that seraphim are the princes or nobles of the heavenly court.[4] The seraphim are probably similar to the cherubim, because "the living creatures"—the "beasts" of Revelation 4—seem to be a combination of the cherubim in Ezekiel 1 and the seraphim of Isaiah 6. It could be that the cherubim and the seraphim are the same. In Revelation 4, each of the cherubim has six wings, too, and just like the seraphim of Isaiah 6, they never stop saying, "Holy, holy, holy is the Lord God Almighty" (Rv 4:8).

The twenty-four elders. Revelation 4:4 says that, "Surrounding the throne... were twenty-four elders. They were dressed in white and had crowns of gold on their heads."

Who are these elders? Some Bible teachers think that the number twenty-four, along with the use of the word "elder," symbolizes the patriarchs of the twelve tribes of Israel, representing all the saints in the Old Testament—*plus* the twelve apostles, representing all the saints in the New Testament. And at first reading they sure seem like saints, because they're wearing white robes and crowns of gold.

I agree with other Bible commentators, however, who believe the twenty-four elders are not symbols of Christian people, but that they depict yet another class of angels. I don't see how they can represent God's covenant people, because they seem to be quite distinct from the saints in several passages (Rv 7:11-13; 14:1-3; 19:4-9), and if their number includes the twelve apostles, why doesn't the apostle John, who is writing the book, see himself among them?

Bible scholar Robert Mounce writes, "It seems best to take the twenty-four elders as an exalted angelic order who serve and adore God as the heavenly counterpart to the twenty-four priestly and twenty-four Levitical orders."[5]

In any case, the biblical use of the number twelve—doubled to the number twenty-four—is a symbol of government and judgment, and this is precisely what the twenty-four elders seem to be associated with in each of the passages where they are mentioned.[6] Calling them "elders" also suggests that they are governing angels. Maybe we could think of the twenty-four elders as heavenly senators, angels of God's ruling order.

The *bene ha'elohim*. The Hebrew language has a surprising number of terms which refer either directly or indirectly to angels. I've already introduced you to the most commonly used word, *malak*, which means simply "messenger." But angels are also called mediators, ministers, watchers, hosts, envoys, holy ones, and "the sons of God"—the mysterious *bene ha'elohim*.[7] This takes us into what is probably the most difficult angel passage in the Bible: Genesis 6. In fact, this is one of the most perplexing accounts in the Bible, period. Just before Noah's flood,

> When men began to increase in number on the earth and daughters were born to them, *the sons of God* saw that the daughters of men were beautiful and they married [Hebrew: took them as wives] any of them they chose.... The Nephilim [a word of uncertain meaning translated "giants" in the KJV] were on the earth in those days—and also afterward—when

the sons of God went to the daughters of men and had children by them. They were the heroes of old, men of renown.[8]

What in the world does this mean? As you can well imagine, Bible scholars have discussed and disputed this text endlessly. What makes us think that this may be a reference to angels is the book of Job, which uses the phrase "the sons of God" several times, each in reference to angelic or nonhuman beings. In fact, the New International Version of the Bible, the one I have been using throughout this book, translates the phrase *bene ha'elohim* "angels": "One day *the angels* came to present themselves before the Lord, and Satan also came with them" (Jb 1:6, italics mine. See also Jb 2:1).

What then are we to make of "the sons of God" in Genesis 6? There are really only two basic interpretations. The first: these beings are human beings, perhaps ancient kings and aristocrats. This would probably be the most comfortable explanation, because it would rule out all the peculiar and supernatural implications of this passage.

Yet if we let the Bible speak for itself here (the second interpretation) it really seems to be referring to heavenly, supernatural beings. Fallen angels. Some people would simply dismiss this explanation as bizarre, while others have argued that Genesis 6 could not possibly refer to angelic beings because Jesus said angels in heaven never marry (see Mt 22:29-30; Mk 12:24-25; Lk 20:34-36). The issue here, however, is not marriage, but sexual relations. Could dark angels actually have sexual relations with human beings? Possibly.

I am inclined to believe that the *bene ha'elohim* of Genesis 6 were celestial beings, and that something extraordinary occurred in their relationships with "the daughters of men." We have already seen how angels can appear in "assumed bodies" so human that they ate and drank with their hosts. In Genesis 6, it seems that there were offspring!

CHERUBIM, BEASTS

The strangest collection of celestial beings is found in the books of Ezekiel and Revelation, both of which seem to describe the same heavenly creatures in different terms. Among the myriad of unusual beings depicted in these books, the cherubim stand out as the most glorious and powerful. We've already met the cherubim briefly in an earlier chapter, as guardians of the entrance to the garden of Eden. They are, in fact, the first angels to appear in the Bible, and they are mentioned most frequently as adornment for the golden Ark of the Covenant. There are also many references to the cherubim as ornamentation in the Tabernacle of Moses and the Temple of Solomon.

Ezekiel 1, one of the most astounding chapters in the Bible, describes the cherubim in elaborate detail. Ezekiel, a prophet whom one Bible commentator has characterized as "weird and wonderful," was standing "by the Kebar River in the land of the Babylonians." Toward the north arose a powerful windstorm, "an immense cloud with flashing lightning and surrounded by brilliant light. The center of the fire," as Ezekiel reported it, "looked like glowing metal, and in the fire was what looked like four living creatures" (Ez 1:4-5). *The cherubim!* We know they are the cherubim, because Ezekiel wrote in a later chapter, "Then the cherubim rose upward. These were the living creatures I had seen by the Kebar River" (Ez 10:15).

Ezekiel proceeds to give us the longest, most detailed description of angelic beings in the Bible. "In appearance," he observed,

> their form was that of a man, but each of them had four faces and four wings. Their legs were straight; their feet were like those of a calf and gleamed like burnished bronze. Under their wings on their four sides they had the hands of a man. All four of them had faces and wings, and their wings touched one another....
>
> Their faces looked like this: Each of the four had the face of a man, and on the right side each had the face of a lion, and

on the left the face of an ox; each also had the face of an eagle.
Such were their faces. Their wings were spread out upward;
each had two wings, one touching the wing of another creature on either side, and two wings covering its body.... The
appearance of the living creatures was like burning coals of
fire or like torches. Fire moved back and forth among the
creatures; it was bright, and lightning flashed out of it.

Ezekiel 1:5-14

A parallel but less exact portrait appears in the Book of
Revelation:

In the center, around the throne, were four living creatures,
and they were covered with eyes, in front and in back. The
first living creature was like a lion, the second was like an ox,
the third had a face like a man, the fourth was like a flying
eagle. Each of the four living creatures had six wings and was
covered with eyes all around, even under his wings.

Revelation 4:6-8

It's no wonder the translators of the King James called these
creatures "beasts"! The inadequacy of human language to
describe the exquisite glories of heaven explains the slight differ-
ences in the two accounts. We're not dealing with something
you can photograph!

Why do they have multiple wings? Because they are swift of
flight to carry out the will of God. Why are they covered with
eyes? Because they are highly intelligent and watchful beings.
Nothing escapes their notice. Why the four faces and forms:
lion, ox, man and eagle? One Bible commentary suggests that
these beings have the strength and nobility of a lion (see Ps
103:20), the ability to serve faithfully as an ox (Heb 1:14), the
intelligence of a man (see Lk 15:10), and the watchfulness and
speed of an eagle.[9]

It may be that the cherubim are the highest ranking angels.
At least they seem to be the closest to God. Adorning the tabernacle, the temple, and the sacred Ark, the cherubim have an

immediate and special relationship with the shekinah glory of God. In the throne room of Revelation 4, day and night they never stop saying, "Holy, holy, holy is the Lord God Almighty, who was, and is, and is to come" (Rv 4:8).

We discover the same relationship between the cherubim and God back in Ezekiel 1. The cherubim flash across the sky like bolts of blazing lightning, leading Ezekiel directly into the brightest corner of the universe—the glorious presence of Almighty God. "Then there came a voice from above the expanse over their heads (the cherubim) as they stood with low-ered wings. Above the expanse over their heads was what looked like a throne of sapphire, and high above on the throne was a figure like that of a man" (Ez 1:25-26). But it was God.

On the throne was the appearance of the likeness of the glory of the Lord. Falling on his face, Ezekiel heard God speak: "I'm sending you to the Israelites." The angelic vision carried Ezekiel into the glorious presence of God. And into the will of God for his life. Angelic beings led Ezekiel into God's presence—and then into God's service.

UFOs?

Cherubim. Strange and awesome beings. Stranger still are their "wheels." Ezekiel reported,

> As I looked at the living creatures [the cherubim], I saw a wheel on the ground beside each creature... This was the appearance and structure of the wheels: They sparkled like chrysolite, and all four looked alike. Each appeared to be made like a wheel inter-secting a wheel. As they moved, they would go in any one of the four directions the creatures faced; the wheels did not turn about as the creatures went. Their rims were high and awesome, and all four rims were full of eyes all around.
>
> When the living creatures moved, the wheels beside them moved; and when the living creatures rose from the ground, the wheels also rose. Wherever the spirit would go, they would

go, and the wheels would rise along with them, because the spirit of the living creatures was in the wheels.   Ezekiel 1:15-21

What in the world was Ezekiel seeing? We know he was seeing the glory of God, but it is entirely possible that, as a part of his vision, Ezekiel was witnessing what people today might call an unidentified flying object, a UFO. Even Billy Graham admits that "UFOs are astonishingly angel-like in some of their reported appearances."[10]

In his book on angels, Billy Graham noted that "some Christians, whose views are anchored in a strong commitment to scripture, contend that... UFOs are angels... These people point to certain passages in Isaiah, Ezekiel, Zechariah and the Book of Revelation, and draw parallels to the reports of observers of the alleged UFO appearances."[11]

Personally, I am fairly convinced that UFOs are indeed the manifestation of spirit beings—and for the most part, not the good kind. In a well-researched article in the *Spiritual Counterfeits Journal*, Mark Albrecht and Brooks Alexander[12] report that UFOs are "usually luminous, glowing, and ethereal; they often display blinking lights and powerful, probing searchlights." (Covered with eyes? Like the wheels of the cherubim?) "They are usually silent, but occasionally hum or even roar."

Furthermore, UFOs seem to defy the laws of gravity and physics. Albrecht and Alexander tell us that "their motions and maneuverings are... enigmatic—they have been known to change their shape suddenly; occasionally they 'materialize' as if from nowhere, but more often 'vanish' into thin air in the midst of a sighting. While in view of both human observers and radar instruments, they have performed unbelievable aerial maneuvers, such as ninety-degree turns at speeds of several thousand miles per hour!" Ezekiel put it this way: "As they moved, they would go in any one of the four directions the cherubim faced; the wheels did not turn about as the cherubim went. The cherubim went in whatever direction the head faced, without turning as they went" (Ez 10:11).

Physicist J. Lemairtre, writing in the highly regarded UFO publication *Flying Saucer Review*, summarizes all this, "We can conclude that it is impossible to interpret UFO phenomenon in terms of material spaceships as we conceive of them, that is, in terms of manufactured and self-propelled machines." And John Keel, reported to be one of the most respected researchers in this field, noted that "over and over again, witnesses have told me in hushed tones, 'You know, I don't think that the thing I saw was mechanical at all. I got the distinct impression that it was *alive*.'" How close to what Ezekiel observed, "The spirit of the living creatures was in the wheels" (Ez 1:15-21).

Another physicist believes that UFOs only appear as matter, but are really just a concentration of energy.[13] All of this points to a spiritual basis for UFO sightings, some of which may be the good angels of God, like what Ezekiel saw near the Kebar River in Babylon.

But most of the time, I believe, UFO sightings are the manifestations of angels of darkness. My main reason for thinking this is that UFO sightings have never, at least to my knowledge, led a person closer to God. In fact, most UFO experiences have just the opposite effect.

Probably the most bizarre UFO sightings are those involving alleged "abductions." Seeing a UFO is one thing. Visiting one or meeting its flight crew is what UFO observers call "a close encounter of the third kind."

The Brian Scott case is perhaps the most famous. He claims to have met the occupants of UFOs on at least five different occasions, in the Superstition Mountains in Arizona. After a bizarre physical examination, the large, weird-looking beings[14] inside the craft communicated with Scott telepathically, without moving their mouths or speaking. The message was a combination of general information about the aliens' origin and purpose, vague philosophy, and a promise that they would return. Which they did.

In subsequent encounters, Scott found himself being used as a channel to reveal secrets of science and metaphysics, most notably a design for a "free psychic energy machine," which would enable all humankind to have the same thought at the same moment! All of this, of course, is blatantly occultic. UFO encounters like this seem to have consistently religious overtones, but unlike Ezekiel's "whirling wheels," UFO beings never lead people into the glorious presence of the Living God.

I believe that UFOs are close encounters of the wrong kind. Prominent French physicist Jacques Vallee observed, "I believe that when we speak of UFO sightings as instances of space visitations we are looking at the phenomenon on the wrong level. We are not dealing with successive waves of visitations from space. We are dealing with a control system... UFOs are the means through which man's concepts are being rearranged."

What you don't know *can* hurt you. The study of UFOs is another sobering reminder that everything we understand in life must be solidly grounded in the teachings of the Bible.

Strange and unusual angels. The angel of the Lord. Archangels. Michael and Gabriel. The *bene ha'elohim*. Cherubim and UFOs. The seraphim. The twenty-four elders. In the chapter that follows, we're going to look into the strangest of the strange, a cosmic paradox: angels from hell.

CHAPTER NINE

Hell's Angels

...Behold the throne of Chaos, and his dark pavillion spread wide on the wasteful deep. **Milton**

Hell is not a pretty sight. But you'd never know it, because Satan and his demons put on a great show. "Satan himself," Paul warns us, "masquerades *as an angel of light*" (2 Cor 11:14, italics mine). Perhaps he's so good at it because he was one. Satan, most Bible scholars believe, was at one time a great angel, perhaps the highest angel in the celestial hierarchy. His actual origin and the specific events that led to his fall are shrouded in mystery. We know much more about what he does than how he got here.

A malignant being... subtle and full of hate.

Donald Grey Barnhouse

THE PRINCE OF DARKNESS IN A COSTUME OF LIGHT

As we have already seen in Chapter 2, the best known passage about the undoing of the devil is found in Isaiah 14:12 "How you have fallen from heaven, O morning star, son of the dawn!" "Lucifer," which is found in the King James Version of this verse, is the Latin word for the planet Venus, known as the morning star because of its bright visibility in the early light of dawn. Ironically, Jesus is also called "the bright Morning Star" (Rv 22:16).

Isaiah 14 continues, "You have been cast down to the earth... You said in your heart, 'I will ascend to heaven; I will raise my throne above the stars [the angels] of God.... I will ascend above the tops of the clouds; I will make myself like the Most High.' But you are brought down to the grave ["sheol" in the Hebrew], to the depths of the pit" (Is 14:12-15).

As I pointed out in Chapter 2, there's a bit of a problem in the way this passage has been understood. In its historical context, Isaiah 14 really refers to the fall of the king of Babylon, or perhaps it's an ancient Canaanite story that Isaiah was using to make his point. And yet some Bible scholars believe that Isaiah 14 also describes Satan's celestial demise—before the beginning of human history. We know something like this must have happened because "that ancient serpent called the devil" (Rv 12:9) was already maliciously interfering with God's purposes in Genesis 3 after the Bible opened with creation in Genesis 1 and Adam and Eve in Genesis 2.

Ezekiel 28 is another key passage about an ancient ruler, the king of Tyre, who is identified as "the anointed cherub."

You were the model of perfection,
    full of wisdom and perfect in beauty.
You were in Eden,
    the garden of God...
You were anointed as *a guardian cherub*,
    for so I ordained you.

You were on the holy mount of God;
　　you walked among the fiery stones.
You were blameless in your ways
　　from the day you were created
　　till wickedness was found in you...
So I drove you in disgrace from the mount of God,
　　and I expelled you, *O guardian cherub*,
　　from among the fiery stones.
Your heart became proud on account of your beauty,
　　and you corrupted your wisdom because of your splendor.
So I threw you to the earth;
　　I made a spectacle of you before kings...
　　you have come to a horrible end and will be no more.

Ezekiel 28:12-19

This passage may be reporting the fall of the devil. If, in fact, it is about Satan, we learn that he was an angel of high position, "anointed as a guardian cherub... on the holy mount of God." And he was sinless, too, "blameless" in all his ways, but wickedness born of pride (same as in Isaiah 14) turned up in his heart and turned him against God. And God turned him out of heaven.

Near the end of the Bible, we read a similar account: "There was war in heaven. Michael and his angels fought against the dragon, and the dragon and his angels fought back. But he was not strong enough, and they lost their place in heaven. The great dragon was hurled down—that ancient serpent called the devil, or Satan, who leads the whole world astray. He was hurled to the earth, and his angels with him" (Rv 12:7-9).

Revelation 9, which begins with classic biblical symbolism, is parallel: "A star [remember the biblical association between angels and stars]... had fallen from the sky to the earth." Undoubtedly, the early Christians would have understood this to be a symbol of the fallen angel, Satan. "The star was given the key to the shaft of the Abyss"—the elevator to hell. As the Abyss opened, there was such an outpouring of darkness that the sun and sky vanished. It was the gloom of one of the most dreaded plagues of the ancient world—a murky, swirling cloud of locusts. But these insects were terribly different: "They were told not to harm... any plant or tree, but only those people who did not have the seal of God on their foreheads" (Rv 9:4).

Instead, they tortured the ungodly with stings *like scorpions*—a symbol of demon power. Jesus explained this earlier in the New Testament: "I saw Satan fall like lightning from heaven. I have given you authority to trample on *snakes* and *scorpions* [the devil and his demons] and to overcome all the power of the enemy" (Lk 10:18-19, italics mine).

To summarize, it's not crystal clear in Scripture exactly where Satan came from, or precisely when he fell to the earth, but that there is a devil, a superhuman opponent of God and his people, is indisputable. His name, *Satan*, means "adversary." The Jews of antiquity also called him by the lesser-known name, *Mastema*—Hebrew for "enmity." In the ancient Qumran scrolls, the devil is "*the angel* of enmity." "Judaism... considered Satan or Mastema to be the incarnation of the principle of hostility to both God and mankind and the regent of all evil spirits."[1] Four times the New Testament calls him "the prince of demons."

Satan's other well-known name is *the devil*, which means "accuser" or "deceiver." It's his title. It's what he does. The devil is also known as:

- the Wicked or Evil One (Mt 6:13)
- the Enemy (Mt 13:25, 28, 39)
- Murderer (Jn 8:44)
- Deceiver (Rv 20:10)
- Beelzebub (Mt 9:34; 12:24)[2]
- Belial, or Beliar, "worthless one" (2 Cor 6:15)
- Ruler of this World (Jn 12:31)• Prince of this world (Jn 12:31)
- Prince of the Power of the Air (Eph 2:2; 6:12)
- the Great Dragon (Rv 12:9)

- the Ancient Serpent (Rv 12:9)
- Abaddon, Apollyon, the Destroyer (Rv 9:11)
- the Tempter (Mt 4:3)

He's the father of lies (Jn 8:44). That's why he's so good at disguising himself as an angel. He's the Prince of Darkness in a costume of light.

A DEVIL OF A BUSINESS

The Devil is in a terrible business. He does every bad thing imaginable. And a lot of other things that look very good. His motives are pride and hate. His strategy is deception. He is in the business of opposing God and resisting the saints. In his excellent book *Angels: Elect and Evil,* C. Fred Dickason has carefully outlined the work of the devil.[3] *In relation to God* he is the adversary of God's person and God's program. *In relation to the nations,* he deceives them through the subtle influence of their governments.

In relation to people who are not Christians, Satan obstructs or distorts the saving message of Jesus. According to the parable of the sower (Lk 8:12), he snatches away the gospel like birds cleaning up grain spilled on the highway.

Somehow this involves insidious mind games, as the apostle Paul explains, "Even if our gospel is veiled, it is veiled to those who are perishing. The god of this age [that is, the devil] has blinded the minds of unbelievers, so that they cannot see the light of the gospel of the glory of Christ" (2 Cor 4:3-4).

Satan accomplishes this by fostering false religions—something the apostle Paul called "the doctrines of demons" (1 Tm 4:1-3)—and by nurturing a godless lifestyle—living without regard to God or his law. Paul's comments about this are explicit: "As for you, you were dead in your transgressions and sins, in which you used to live when you followed the ways of this world and of the ruler of the kingdom of the air, the spirit who is now at work in those who are disobedient" (Eph 2:1-3).

Finally, *in relation to Christians,* the devil fights us tooth and nail: "Put on God's complete armor so that you can successfully resist all the devil's methods of attack. For our fight is not against any physical enemy: it is against... the unseen power that controls this dark world, and spiritual agents from the very headquarters of hell" (Eph 6:11-12, PHILLIPS). The "devil's methods of attack" include accusing and slandering—the very meaning of his name (Rv 12:10). And planting doubt. Tempting us to sin. Inciting persecution. Standing in the way of the ministry: "Brothers," Paul wrote, "we wanted to come to you—certainly I, Paul, did again and again—*but Satan stopped us*" (1 Thes 2:18).

Probably Satan's most successful schemes are the most subtle: misunderstanding in relationships and the deeply painful divisions that result—church splits, litigation between friends and neighbors, runaway children, divorce. You can read a litany of the devil's success on the front page of today's newspaper.

It's often overlooked that Ephesians 6, perhaps the most familiar Bible passage about spiritual warfare, is really about people problems and how the devil uses them to achieve his diabolical purposes. Just before the famous passage on the armor of God in Ephesians 6, Paul addresses all kinds of relationship scenarios: husbands and wives (Eph 5:22-33), children and parents (Eph 6:1-4), and slaves and masters, or in our culture, as the *Living Bible* suggests, employers and employees (Eph 6:5-9).

Then, and only then, does Paul demand, "Finally, be strong in the Lord and in his mighty power. Put on the full armor of God.... For our struggle *is not against flesh and blood*" (Eph 6:10-12). That is, your struggles are *not* with all the people in your life that you think are your big problems. Life's battles are on a much deeper level, and your problems are not just with other people, but with the principalities and powers of darkness who work behind the scenes to disrupt all our important relationships—husbands and wives, children and parents, employers and employees.

Before we move on to consider demons and what they do, I

want to clarify one more important issue. Satan may be the *second* most powerful being in the universe, *but he is not omnipo-tent.* His power and authority fall well below the throne of God. Paul reminds us that Christ is seated at the right hand of the Father, "*far above* all rule and authority, power and dominion, and every title that can be given, not only in the present age but also in the one to come" (Eph 1:21).

Satan isn't omnipresent either. He's a fallen angel, a finite being. As an angel, he probably has "wings," in the sense that he can move swiftly from one place in time and space to another. But unlike God, he is not everywhere at once. You would think he is, though, by the way people talk about him. He *seems* to be everywhere at once, but that's part of the illusion. What seems like the devil to most people is probably nothing more than demons, bitterly serving their wicked master.

In summary, the devil functions as a kind of negative universe: whatever God is for, the devil's against it. Satan is the embodiment of evil, and he has a myriad of fallen angels to assist him.

WHERE DO DEMONS COME FROM?

Not all the angels are good. *Daimones* is the Greek word for demons. According to the Bible, demons, who collaborate with the devil himself, are an evil third (Rv 12:3-4) of the population of the spirit realm. Who are the demons? And where did they come from? The quick and easy answer is that they are fallen ("dark") angels. And that's what I believe, but it might surprise you that not everyone feels this way. C. Fred Dickason admits that "there is a question concerning the origin and identification of demons... because the Bible does not specifically settle the issue."[4] And theologian Henry Theissen called it "a perplexing question."

Fallen angels. The first theory, and the one I accept along with the great majority of Bible teachers, *is that demons are legions of fallen angels.* These are dysfunctional angels, serving the devil and making life miserable for human beings. There are several reasons for believing this view. First, there are parallel expressions like "the devil and his angels" (Mt 25:41) and "Beelzebub, the prince of demons" (Mt 12:24ff). It's obvious that the terms here are interchangeable, that the "devil" and "Beelzebub" are the same. So are "his angels" and "demons." I should point out, though, that Satan, who is a fallen angel, is never called a demon. Second, angels and demons seem to have the same nature. Both are called "spirits."[5] Third, both demons and evil angels carry out the same terrible work, joining with Satan to oppose God and man.

Disembodied spirits of a "lost civilization." The second theory is that demons are the disembodied spirits of a pre-Adamic race. In other words, some Bible scholars have speculated that a race of human beings existed *before* the creation of Adam and Eve. They base their view on what appears to be a *re*-creation of the earth in Genesis 1: "In the beginning... the earth was formless, and darkness was over the surface of the waters."

Why, they ask, was the earth formless and dark? Why is there the suggestion of chaos? We know that God created everything out of *nothing*, but in Genesis 1, it seems like God started over with *something* and rearranged it. Maybe there was a race of beings living on the earth before Adam—a race of beings that destroyed the "first" earth. And maybe the devil was involved with this somehow.

Well, we just don't know. We don't have videotape of Creation! The first chapter of Genesis tells us the whole creation account, but leaves out a lot of details. What the formless darkness means at the beginning of Genesis 1 is one of those things. Furthermore, there is no other place anywhere in the Bible that even remotely suggests the existence of a pre-Adamic race. I am convinced, then, that this is *not* where the demons came from.

The spirits of the *bene ha'elohim*. A third theory, something we touched on in the previous chapter, is that the demons are the offspring of the "sons of God" and the daughters of men in

Genesis 6. Apparently the early Christian writer Justin believed this. In the second century he wrote, "God committed the care of men and all things under heaven to angels whom he appointed over them. But the angels transgressed this appointment, and were captivated by the love of the women, and begot children who are those that are called demons."[6] This view has not been widely held by Christian leaders. In my view, it's pure conjecture. In light of the enormous amount of demonic activity that seems evident in our world today, those "sons of God" would have had to have an impossible number of offspring.

Disembodied spirits of the departed. The fourth theory is that demons are the disembodied spirits of the wicked dead. "The damned sent back to haunt the living," as one writer put it.[7] In other words, when evil people die, their spirits are released to wander the earth until the day of judgment. This was the view of the ancient Jewish writers Philo and Josephus, and surprisingly, many of the early Christian authors. It is believed these roaming ghosts, or "manes," haunt old houses and dark forests—and possess the souls and bodies of those who are living.

Some people even believe that the souls of the departed watch over them and protect them like the angels. Sophy Burnham reports in her book, "I heard of one German woman who was in a terrible car accident ten days after her husband died.... She attributes her survival to the protection of her husband.... because she felt his presence so powerfully at the crash."[8]

But the insurmountable problem with this theory is that it just isn't in the Bible. Anywhere. God's Word does teach, however, that the departed souls of ungodly people go into a temporary prison of death called "sheol" or "hades," while the spirits of the righteous dead go into the presence of God. *Sheol* is a Hebrew word; *hades* is Greek. Both terms mean essentially the same thing: an intermediate dwelling place of the dead.

Hell is different. It's final and forever, and contrary to popular opinion, ungodly people don't go straight to hell. According to Revelation, hell does not open its gates until *after* the last judgment:

The dead were judged according to what they had done as recorded in the books. The sea gave up the dead that were in it, *and death and hades* gave up the dead that were in them, and each person was judged according to what he had done. *Then death and hades* were thrown into the lake of fire. The lake of fire is the second death.   **Revelation 20:13-14 (italics mine)**

So for now, according to Scripture, ungodly people go straight to sheol, or hades. Not that they get a second chance there. Hades is a holding cell before final sentencing when God appears on his Great White Throne of judgment.

Even some of the fallen angels are jailed there, as Jude reveals: "And the angels who did not keep their positions of authority, but abandoned their own home—these he has kept in darkness, bound with everlasting chains for judgment on the great Day" (Jude 6).

Why some of the fallen angels are bound and others are on parole is not clear, but Peter, too, declares, "For... God did not spare the angels when they sinned, but sent them to hell [Greek: *tartarus*], putting them into gloomy dungeons *to be held for judgment*" (2 Pt 2:4, italics mine). *Tartarus* was the worst of the worst, the deepest of the deep, the darkest and most dreadful grotto in hades.[9]

For all these reasons, demons cannot be the disembodied spirits of ungodly dead people. There is absolutely no teaching in the New Testament about the wandering spirits of the dead or ghosts.

THE DANGER OF TALKING WITH THE DEAD

As a student of the Bible, I have to believe that reports of the actual souls of the departed revisiting the living probably have their basis in some demonic activity, perhaps a demon in the disguise of a loved one. I believe it is possible, however, on extraordinary occasions, that the Lord might use a vision—not the actual spirit of the person—to let us know that a deceased loved one is at peace in God's presence in heaven.

My wife, Marilyn, had a rare experience like that a few days after her mother died. In an unexpected, trance-like moment, a thousand miles away from her mother's grave, Marilyn "saw" the unspeakably joyful face of her mom. It was so real that, years later, my wife still can't talk about it without crying.

For a fleeting moment, it seems that God opened heaven and permitted my wife to see how happy and well-cared for her mother was, there with him. Neither of us, though, had any sense that Marilyn's mom had somehow returned from the dead to revisit us, or that she had some message for us from beyond the grave. Her mother didn't speak to her. She didn't even look at her! Marilyn just saw her face.

The Bible, I think, leaves a very slight crack in the door between the living and the dead. In the Gospel accounts, James, Peter, and John saw Moses and Elijah, long-departed Old Testament saints, talking with Jesus on the mountain of Christ's transfiguration. The dead, we learn from this, are not really dead. But we also have to notice how Moses and Elijah never said a word to the apostles. In fact, they didn't even seem to acknowledge their presence. Jesus—not the disembodied spirits of Moses and Elijah—is the center of the account and the focus of everyone's attention. Jesus is the only link between heaven and earth, the ladder upon whom angels ascend and descend (Jn 1:51). Jesus is our intermediary, not a medium.

The Bible expressly forbids the use of mediums or any direct contact with the dead: "When you enter the land the Lord your God is giving you, do not learn to imitate the detestable ways of the nations there. Let no one be found among you... who is a medium or spiritist or who consults the dead" (Dt 18:9, 11). On an even harsher note, Moses warned the people of Israel, "A man or woman who is a medium or spiritist among you must be put to death. You are to stone them; their blood will be on their own heads" (Lv 20:27).

In spite of the many perplexities which plague our understanding of Satan and his evil forces, it does seem to be indisputable that he exists. And that he himself contributes to the confusion surrounding the realm of darkness.

"Demon" is a synonym for "dark angel." But what do dark angels do for a living? This is the subject of my next chapter.

CHAPTER TEN

What Dark Angels Do for a Living

The world of demons, fallen angels, is very real—a fact we need to know. We have to face up to this terrible reality, so that we do not fall unsuspectingly into their hands and come under their tyranny. **Basilea Schlink**

Dark angels are servants of Satan. Where Satan leads, demons follow. What we said of Satan's work in the last chapter could be said with equal confidence about the demons. Together they cooperate in a celestial conspiracy against God, God's purposes, and God's people. Sometimes referred to as evil spirits, demons appear throughout the pages of the Bible. More and more people today believe that demons are real, actively disrupting people's lives.

Recently, I spoke with an acquaintance who is a marriage and family therapist in the Seattle area. In November 1993 she was a participant in the Institute of Advanced Clinical Training in Washington, D.C., attended by over four thousand counselors and therapists. Hot issues were ritual abuse, multiple personality disorders, and repressed memory therapy. In an informal, spontaneous survey, one of the plenary speakers asked the huge gathering, "How many of you believe in the real existence of an evil force or demons?" The vast majority, perhaps as many as 80% according to my friend, raised their hands.

Demons are real. Demons are seductive and nasty. According to the Bible, demons energize human immorality and wickedness (1 Cor 10:20; Rv 9:20-21), cause some illnesses and many other forms of human suffering (Lk 8:30; 13:11), are the instigators of idolatry and false religion (Acts 16:16; 1 Cor 10:20; 1 Tm 4:1; 1 Jn 4:1-2, 6), and may exercise influence over world governments (Eph 6:12; Dn 10:13). Probably their most commonly known crime is breaking and entering—literally possessing the bodies of living humans.

Like Satan and good angels, demons are not omnipresent. There are many of them, so they are all around us, but no one demon, no matter how powerful, can be more than one place at the same time. In other words, demons are local, and it seems that they are able to influence a single person, object, or place, often for long periods of time. Demons, then, may be found haunting buildings or other specific locales; associating themselves with material objects or possessing animals; oppressing families, perhaps for generations; possessing people by entering their bodies, something commonly called "demonization"; or exercising hellish influence over nations, regions, geographical territories, and cities.

HAUNTED PLACES

I don't believe in friendly ghosts; I don't believe in ghosts, period. I believe that what people think of as ghosts are in fact demon spirits—no matter how pleasant, helpful, or innocuous some apparition may seem.

We hear stories about harmless ghosts in old buildings. Here in Arizona, there is reputed to be a friendly spirit in a particular room in an old, turn-of-the-century hotel in Arizona's territorial capital. The principal Phoenix newspaper, *The Arizona Republic*, headlined last year: "Believe in ghosts? Nineteen percent polled in Arizona do." The caption under an eerie photo on the front page read, "The Hotel Vendome in Prescott supposedly is haunted by a ghost named Abby. 'It gets plenty weird around here sometimes,' says Mark Payne, assistant manager at the hotel."[1]

Is this possible? Yes. Is this demonic? I believe so. A couple of years ago, my wife and I stayed in a bed and breakfast in Massachusetts. The proprietor seemed so nice on the phone, and she was no less pleasant when she greeted us at the door of her home in the murky twilight of a crisp October evening. Once inside, though, the spiritual air was clammy and suffocating. The house, over three hundred years old, was gorgeously decorated with period antiques, but the feeling inside was almost more oppressive than I could bear. Now I didn't see any ghosts—or demons—but there was an unmistakable, spiritual presence in that home.

Surprisingly, the Bible does not address the issue of haunted places. Jesus comes close when he speaks of demon possession in Luke 11:24: "When an evil spirit comes out of a man, it goes through arid places seeking rest and does not find it."

IDOLS AND MAGIC OBJECTS

Dark angels also seem to associate themselves with material objects. This is the root of idolatry. There are a couple of

Hebrew words which can refer to demon spirits: *sedim,* which means "lords," and *elilim,* which means "idols." Very early in their history, the Jewish people regarded idolatrous images as mere visible symbols of invisible demons (see Dt 32:17; Ps 96:5).

The apostle Paul concludes, "The sacrifices of pagans are offered to demons.... You cannot drink the cup of the Lord and the cup of demons too; you cannot have a part in both the Lord's table and the table of demons" (1 Cor 10:20-21). Specifically, Paul is discouraging Christians from eating meat that had been offered as sacrifices in pagan temples, because of its close association with demons.

This is undoubtedly the explanation for the power in religious objects, relics, icons, statues, amulets, charms, and fetishes. Most of the time, I think that a physical object has spiritual power only to the degree that we believe it does. In other words, if an object of the occult—a jack-o-lantern, let's say—is not revered as a religious object, then it has no power, no matter how religious-like the object may be. Carving a pumpkin face in the autumn doesn't automatically mean that you are opening up your life and home to evil spirits.

On the other hand, some objects may have some association with spiritual power. In October 1993, I participated in an international consultation on spiritual warfare in Seoul, Korea. In a more light-hearted moment between intense conference sessions, I talked with some of the Asian delegates about shopping for souvenirs.

One of the Christian brothers from Malaysia suddenly turned serious. "You Americans," he warned me, "have to be careful about what kind of souvenirs you carry home with you. Many of the objects sold in the tourist shops here in Asia have religious significance. They've been prayed over and consecrated to heathen gods."

Not too long ago George Otis, who has studied spiritual phenomena all over the world, introduced me to an intriguing book about music and spiritual power written by Mickey Hart, for years the drummer for the rock group the "Grateful Dead." The book, *Drumming at the Edge of Magic: A Journey into the Spirit of Percussion*, is a history of the drum from a spiritualistic perspective. Probably the single most captivating section of the book is about a Tibetan ritual drum called a *damaru*. "The most distinctive *damarus*," Hart tells us, "are made from human skulls." He continues, "In twenty years of drum collecting I've possessed only two *damarus*.... This first *damaru* nearly killed me."[2]

A friend, who bought the drum in India, gave it to Hart, knowing that the famous drummer would "appreciate its power." Well, when he finally pulled it down from his shelf to give it a few thumps, he was really disappointed by its boring sound. "I never expected to play it again," he writes. "I set it back on a shelf and then went and threw up. I had no reason to associate my nausea with the *damaru*. But I soon began bumping into things, falling down when I shouldn't have, injuring myself in minor but annoying ways; it gradually felt as if everything in my life was beginning to unravel."[3]

Hart finally decided to return the drum to a Tibetan Buddhist center in Berkeley. "So you've come home at last," the head lama said, looking at the drum. Then he turned to Hart: "I hope you have been most careful, Mickey Hart. This is a drum of great, great power. It wakes the dead, you know."[4]

Somehow, dark angels have the power to energize lifeless objects with the goal of enticing people to worship or serve the object instead of the God of heaven. "Transmogrification," more commonly known as "poltergeist" (German for "noisy ghost"), is an uncommon term that refers to strange movements or bizarre changes in inanimate objects, like banging doors or bleeding icons.

In an earlier chapter, I referred to an article in the *Spiritual Counterfeits Journal* about the reality and nature of UFOs. Some of the same concepts apply here. In the article, Dr. Curt Wagner, a physicist with a Ph.D. in general relativity, states that "it seems that supernatural forces can manipulate matter and energy, extracting energy from the atmosphere, to manipulate matter and produce an apparent violation [of the laws of physics]."[5] In other words, an idol or icon that speaks and does other enticing tricks is scientifically plausible.

Here's a real story,[6] a remarkable and frightening illustration of demon activity. (If you are uncomfortable reading about demon activity, I suggest you skip over the next few paragraphs, although the account has a "happy ending.")

As far back as I can remember I had nightmares about being awake in bed, unable to open my eyes, move, or speak. Eventually these nightmares turned into something much more terrifying: a demon clothed in a hooded black cloak began to appear. This same being has shown itself to several female members of our family [I discuss family spirits later in this chapter.—Author], and we have argued about whether the being itself is male or female.

This demon often entered our night dreams and would say horrible things. At times, we could even feel its physical touch. Rarely has any of us in the family been able to take a nap during the day, because for whatever reason, it has *always* appeared to us at those times.

When I moved to Arizona in 1986, away from my family, some other very unusual things began to happen in addition to the nightmares. Doors would open and close when no one was in that part of the house. For example, on one occasion my daughter, who was fifteen at the time, was alone in her room. For some reason unknown to us, her bedroom door lock was on the *outside* of the door. While she was sitting on her bed doing homework—and I was in the living room reading—her door suddenly slammed shut and locked by itself.

Another time, when my daughter was seventeen, she told me she had seen little, black, shadowy figures dancing on the patio, and it frightened her terribly.

Meanwhile, my nightmares were becoming more frequent, with added migraine headaches. I was still not a Christian, and God was beginning to draw me to himself. Even though I had been raised in a Christian home, and I knew I needed to be saved, I was living my life without God—and paying the price.

One night I was home alone, and there were many strange shuffling noises in the house—and a terribly evil atmosphere. I have never experienced such fear. Having this overwhelming sense that someone was watching me, I tried to shake the feeling by going to bed. But when I went into the bathroom to wash my face, the feeling intensified. Sitting on my bathroom counter was a glass jar full of cotton balls. As I was standing there, right before my eyes, the lid on that jar raised into the air, hovered there for a split second, and then crashed and broke into a million pieces.

As you can well imagine, I could not sleep that night. All I could do was lie there in sheer terror, unable to resist the darkness. I had been lying there for only a few minutes, when I felt a cold breeze blowing in my room. I was awake and my eyes were open. The moon was shining brightly through my window.

Suddenly, that familiar figure, dressed in its black, hooded cloak, "walked" into my room. I was paralyzed with fear. "If 'she' looks at me directly," I thought, "I'm going to die." The being passed right by my bed and disappeared into the bathroom. After my heart stopped pounding and I could breathe easier, I slipped out of bed and peered cautiously into the bathroom. But there was nothing there. Shaking, I went back to bed and, thankfully, fell asleep.

A few months later, I gave my heart to Christ and made him Lord of my life. It happened at a women's retreat, where for the first time I learned about things like generational curses and deliverance. I told some of the women at the retreat about the hooded visitor, and they laid hands on me and prayed. I had no more nightmares for several months!

But then one night, the dark being reappeared. I was asleep, and the old nightmare—and the feeling of helpless paralysis—returned. I actually found myself wrestling physically with the hooded figure—at least that was the impression I had in my dream. But deliverance came when I started shouting, "I resist you in the name of Jesus." The terrible thing fled, and it has never returned! That was two years ago.

A footnote on the story: Not long ago, I was flipping through a mail order catalog of New Age and occult products. I was stunned when I saw an illustration of small cast statue for sale—an exact image of the hooded being in my nightmares. It was called "Queen of the Middle Earth." I also learned recently that an ancestor on my mother's side was heavily involved in witchcraft.

Dark angels, it seems, have the capacity to associate themselves—and even move—inanimate objects (see Ex 7:10-12), but let me sound a word of caution here. You don't have to start throwing things out of your house tonight. Not everything made by the hands of those involved in other religions is dedicated directly to the devil or is demon-empowered, but we should be wary and discerning.

Some objects, however, because of their potential spiritual significance, simply do not belong in the homes of Christians. And you probably shouldn't sell them at a swap meet, or give them away. In Acts, "Many of those who believed now came and openly confessed their evil deeds. A number who had practiced sorcery brought their scrolls together and burned them publicly" (Acts 19:18-19).

DEMONIZATION

The Bible is very plain on the subject of demonization, that evil spirits have the ability to enter the bodies of living people and control their thoughts, emotions, and actions. The Lord Jesus himself believed that demons play a significant role in certain human behaviors, and that they must be driven out (Mt 4:23-24).

Demons on occasion possess human bodies. This is probably

one of the reasons why some people believe that demons are the disembodied spirits of the dead, desperate to return to the land of the living. I have already explained that demons are not ghosts of the dead. They're dark angels, part of a grand scheme to disrupt and control God's creation.

Matthew and Dennis Linn have taught on healing in many countries and universities, including a course for doctors accredited by the American Medical Association. In the introduction to their book *Deliverance Prayer*, Matthew Linn confesses his previous struggle to believe in the reality of demons today:

> Ten years ago I could not have [written] this book. I knew that Christ called us to preach, heal and cast out demons in his name (Mk 6:12-13; 16:15-18). I was willing to do the first two but didn't believe at all in demons. My graduate studies in anthropology, psychology and theology convinced me that demons were only to be found as gargoyles on medieval cathedrals or fantasies created by too much demon rum....
>
> A growing number of doctors, psychiatrists and social workers now know that it is sometimes as necessary to treat demonic bondage with deliverance prayer as it is to treat bacteria with penicillin, a manic depressive neurosis with therapy and drugs, or an alcoholic with AA and environmental change.
>
> Through the Association of Christian Therapists I have come to know over twelve hundred professionals who combine healing power, of which deliverance is a small but important part.[7]

Many credible people agree. Best-selling author M. Scott Peck devotes an entire chapter of his book *People of the Lie* to deliverance ministry. He is convinced, as a practicing psychiatrist, that the most difficult human problems, particularly those associated with denial and addictive behaviors, are energized by demon power.

Intertwining themselves with the personality of their victim, demons can control to one degree or another various aspects of the person's life. In his landmark book *Demon Possession and the Christian*, C. Fred Dickason defines demonization as "demon-caused passivity or control due to a demon's residing within a person, which manifests its effect in various physical and mental disorders and in varying degrees."[8]

Why the dark angels have such an obsession for possession is not clear, particularly in view of the fact that good angels seem to have no interest whatsoever in indwelling human bodies. A possible explanation has occurred to me. Godly people are actually indwelt by the *Holy* Spirit as a representative of the God whom they serve. Christianity is not just a religious belief system. It's relationship and communion with the living God. It is Christ *in us*, the hope of glory.

In a perverted attempt to counterfeit this wonderful relationship Christians have with God, Satan vicariously indwells great numbers of people by sending his *evil* spirits, his dark angels, into their bodies. The Holy Spirit, as the Third Person of the Trinity, is omnipresent. He can indwell an unlimited number of people, changing their hearts and guiding their lives. The devil, on the other hand, is not omnipresent. As powerful as he is, he can only possess and control one person at a time. Hence the need for legions of fallen angels to carry out his malevolent strategy to influence and dominate as many human beings as he possibly can.

Dark angels, then, may enter and control the lives of human persons, although how much they can "possess" a person's life is a matter of debate. Charles Kraft, in his excellent book *Defeating Dark Angels: Breaking Demonic Oppression in the Believer's Life*, reminds us that the term "demon possessed" is based on a poor translation of the Greek work *daimonizomai*, which, more precisely, means "demonized," or "under the influence of a demon." Another phrase found a few times in the New Testament is *echein daimonion*, which means simply "to have a demon."

"It is far better," Kraft writes, "to use a more neutral term such as 'have a demon' or 'demonized.' Both are more true to the original Greek and also run less risk of frightening people."

Even the famous Bible scholar Merrill Unger recognized that the term "demon possession," such a popular term today, does not appear in the Bible.[9] Charles Kraft concludes that "demons cannot totally control a person all the time, though in severe demonization, nearly total control may occur for shorter or longer periods of time."[10]

A popular myth is that Christians cannot be demon possessed. Technically, that's true. Christians are possessed—owned, if you will—by the Holy Spirit, so Christian believers could never be completely demon "possessed." But if we understand that demon "possession" should be more generally understood as demonization or demon influence, then yes, it seems possible for a Christian believer to be personally oppressed by dark angels. Dickason has made a case for the demonization of Christians in his persuasive book *Demon Possession and the Christian*.

In her classic 1912 work on demons, *War on the Saints*, Jesse Penn-Lewis purports that

> Christians are as open to possession by evil spirits as other men, and become possessed because they have, in most cases, *unwittingly fulfilled the conditions upon which evil spirits work....* The primary cause of deception and possession in believers may be condensed into one word, *Passivity:* that is, a cessation of the active exercise of the will in control over spirit, soul, and body.[11]

DELIVERANCE

It is a bit out of the focus of this book for me to deal at length with this aspect of dark angels. For those who are particularly interested in deliverance ministry—how to do it and what to watch out for—several very good Christian books are available.[12] But since I have poked into the issue, I probably should give you some basic advice.

Michael Scanlan and Randall J. Cirner[13] are wise to suggest that deliverance can occur on different levels. According to these authors, "personal or self-deliverance" is often possible through significant growth in personal holiness, or a person might minister to himself by commanding the dark angels to leave in the name of Jesus. Peter warns us, "Be self-controlled and alert. Your enemy the devil prowls around like a roaring lion looking for someone to devour. *Resist him, standing firm in the faith*" (1 Pt 5:8-9, italics mine).

Secondly, "fraternal deliverance" is when God works through Christian brothers and sisters to minister release from spiritual oppression. This is the everyday kind of deliverance, as James commands us, "Confess your sins to each other and pray for each other so that you may be healed" (Jas 5:16).

The third type of deliverance is "pastoral." According to Scanlan and Cirner, "When a person has pastoral responsibility for other people, the Lord gives that person the gifts and the authority to deal with deeper and more complex workings of evil spirits."

Fourth is "special ministry." We must acknowledge that God has given to some people special gifts of discernment, revelation, and authority to overcome Satan and dark angels at their most profound level of activity. Personally, I have confronted and cast out demons on several occasions, but this is not my primary ministry gift. I'd rather preach a sermon or write a book! I can deal with evil spirits if it's necessary, but I prefer to refer more difficult cases to people who are more gifted and more patient.

How do you cast out a demon? A few tips in a short chapter like this are hardly adequate to deal with such a complex and explosive subject, but there are some general guidelines I think everyone should understand. In my book on spiritual warfare, *Overcoming the Dominion of Darkness*, I suggest the following:

First, ask yourself if it is a condition of demonization you can handle. If not, make a referral to someone who is competent in spiritual ministry, or you may wish to ask one or two others to assist you. If you are not sure, ask God if he is leading you to become involved. If God doesn't make it clear to you that you should become involved, don't.

Second, prepare yourself. Pray, asking for the anointing of power and the discerning of spirits. Jesus taught his disciples that some evil spirits do not respond to just anyone, anytime. Some people are delivered from dark angels only after fervent prayer and fasting.

Third, ask the demonized person to prepare for ministry with prayer and fasting. This is not possible, of course, if the individual is heavily oppressed, or if they ask for prayer not knowing that their problems are deeply spiritual.

Fourth, minister deliverance privately whenever possible. If I'm caught off-guard in a public meeting by an unexpected demonic manifestation, I always try to have the demonized person escorted to another room. Demons seem to like attention. Furthermore, observing a deliverance can be very frightening to people who are not familiar with that kind of ministry.

Fifth, in the name of Jesus command the dark angel, by name if necessary, to leave. Remember, the power of God has to do with Christ in you and the Spirit working through you, not the volume of your voice or the intensity of the religious feeling you might have at the moment.

Sixth, invite the Holy Spirit to come and fill the void, so that the dark angel can't take up residence again so easily.

THE LIMITATIONS OF DELIVERANCE

Deliverance is not a cure-all. Not every human problem has a demonic origin. James wrote, "When tempted, no one should say, 'God is tempting me.' For God cannot be tempted by evil, nor does he tempt anyone; but each one is tempted... [not by the devil, but] by his own evil desire" (Jas 1:13-14). In other words, the dark angels may have enormous influence on us. Satan is the Great Tempter. But you can never say, "The devil *made* me do it." Ultimately, each of us is personally responsible for our behaviors.

Matthew Linn writes, "Those who see a need only for deliverance err just as greatly as those who see a need only for medicine, only for psychiatric treatment, or only for environmental change, when several or all of these factors may contribute to a person's suffering."[14] Deliverance, Charles Kraft asserts, is not a one-shot deal.

Deliverance does not always last. I wrote in my book on spiritual warfare that "even when a release from an evil spirit occurs, it does not guarantee permanent freedom. Deliverance must be accompanied by a commitment to obey God's Word and grow in Christ. Sometimes, if not always, personal accountability to other mature Christians is necessary during the healing period. Satan's government must be exchanged for God's, not just cast out."[15] Jesus taught,

> When an evil spirit comes out of a man, it goes through arid places seeking rest and does not find it. Then it says, "I will return to the house I left." When it arrives, it finds the house unoccupied, swept clean and put in order. Then it goes and takes with it seven other spirits more wicked than itself, and they go in and live there. And the final condition of that man is worse than the first.   **Matthew 12:43-45**

Deliverance does not always work. I have prayed for people to be delivered from what appeared to be unmistakably demonic symptoms, and their problems have not gone away. When praying with someone, we need to know not only when to begin, but *when to stop*. There may be other factors that require us to withdraw our forces in order to consider the problem from other angles. Sometimes it is a demon, sometimes it is not. Sometimes we lack faith, other times we don't. Spiritual warfare is serious business, so keep asking God for discernment and power. If there is work to be done, he will show you how to do it.

CAN AN ANIMAL HAVE A DEMON?

This is rare but possible. I have a friend here in the Phoenix area who is a full-time therapist. He has had a lot of experience with ritual abuse and demonization. A couple of years ago, after deliverance prayer for someone in their home, their cat went berserk. The demon, it seemed, entered the body of their pet. When he and his wife prayed for the animal, a second deliverance ensued!

A similar incident occurred in the Gospel of Mark (Mk 5:1ff). Jesus crossed over the Sea of Galilee to the region of the Gerasenes, where he was confronted by a wild man possessed by a legion of demons. "No one was strong enough to subdue him. Night and day among the tombs and in the hills he would cry out and cut himself with stones."

When Jesus saw him, he demanded, "Come out of this man, you evil spirit!"

But the dark angels begged Jesus not to send them out of the region. "Send us, instead, among those pigs over there on the hillside."

Jesus agreed, and the legion of dark angels entered the herd of swine. About two thousand pigs rushed wildly down the steep bank, into the lake, and drowned. Deviled ham!

The whole thing is puzzling. Why would the demons possess the pigs only to kill them? And where did the demons go when the pigs drowned? Some people have suggested that it all had something to do with how Hebrews weren't supposed to be eating pork. What were Jewish people doing, we wonder, in the business of raising swine? Or, perhaps, because this took place in the Decapolis region, a Gentile area, these pigs were being raised for Roman sacrifices.

Whatever else we can learn from the account, we can conclude that demons have the ability to possess the bodies of both men and beasts. But let me repeat my opening line in this section: *demon possession of animals is extremely rare.* It was recorded only once in the Bible, and in all my years of ministry, I've heard of only a handful of similar incidents.

FAMILY SPIRITS

Some families seem to have problems that last for generations, like the story of the hooded being earlier in this chapter. I am persuaded that it's a sinister strategy of dark angels—assigned by Satan—to attach themselves to families and other close associations of people. It is commonly known that family traits and manners are passed along through heredity and environment. Numerous medical, psychological, and sociological studies have shown how problems like alcohol abuse are greatly influenced both by genetics and environmental factors.

But maybe there's more. Admittedly, the Bible is vague on the matter of generational curses, but Scripture does suggest that family sins, or at least their consequences, are passed on for several generations. In the Ten Commandments, God declared, "You shall not bow down to [other gods] or worship them; for I, the Lord your God, am a jealous God, punishing the children for the sin of the fathers to the third and fourth generations."

Family patterns and sins are repeated with uncanny regularity from one generation to the next, while several generations—children and grandchildren—may suffer as the direct result of parental sins.

The social evidence now is overwhelming. "Dan Quayle Was Right," trumpeted the cover of the prestigious *Atlantic Monthly.* "After decades of public dispute about so-called family diversity," the article went on to say, "the evidence from social-science research is coming in: The dissolution of two-parent families, though it may benefit the adults involved, is harmful to many children, and dramatically undermines our society."[16] There is often a direct correlation between "problem children" and the problems of their parents.

Could it be that dark angels are subtly but powerfully escalating the problems? I am inclined to believe it. Husbands and wives "submit to one another out of reverence to Christ.... Children obey your parents.... Fathers, bring your children up in the training and instruction of the Lord.... *For our struggle is not against flesh and blood, but ... against the powers of this dark world and against the spiritual forces of evil in the heavenly realms*" (from Eph 5:21–6:12, italics mine).

It's clear in this passage that the devil attacks the family and other significant relationships. It's only logical to assume—although we have to keep reminding ourselves that the Bible doesn't teach this directly—that specific dark angels are assigned the task of ravaging the same families one generation after another, unless the curse is broken by the power of God. Remember, our life span as human beings is fixed. We top out at a hundred years, at the very most. Dark angels, though, have been around for thousands of years, and they may spend aeons in the same place.

Charles Kraft agrees. He writes,

I cannot understand why God allows this, but children may become demonized [not possessed, but influenced by demons] through heredity. We often refer to this as the passing on of *generational or "bloodline" spirits/power.*

Sometimes one or more spirits are inherited. I have frequently found this to be the case with people whose parents and/or grandparents were in Freemasonry. This is not surprising, since Freemasons regularly curse themselves through secret oaths they take. In the higher degrees, they dedicate themselves and their families to Lucifer.[17]

The same familiar spirits, I believe, may hang around members and descendants of the same families. Similar to the legion of evil spirits in the incident of the pigs from hell, these family spirits beg again and again "not to send them *out of the area*" (Mk 5:10).

Like Jesus, we need to stand up to them and cast them away from us forever. We must recognize Satan's anti-family values and counteract his schemes with the power of the Holy Spirit and an uncompromising commitment to obeying God's word. In bold contrast to the curse on the third and fourth generations, God promises that he will show his love "to a *thousand generations* of those who love me *and keep my commandments*" (Ex 20:6, italics mine).

TERRITORIAL SPIRITS

Dark angels seem to love specific "areas"—geographical places, mountains, and regions. Like human beings and other creatures of God, demons may be territorial. Overtones of territorial spirits appear as early as the fifteenth century B.C., in Canaanite mythology. Each of the ancient gods were said to have had "a dwelling place on a particular sacred mountain, at some inaccessible point where heaven and earth meet. From such mountains their rule over the land and their influence upon its life were believed to flow."[18]

These were the gods of the regions. This is played out in the ancient battle between Ahab, king of Israel, and Ben-Hadad, king of Aram, in 1 Kings 20. The military strategy of the campaign was influenced by the idea of territorial gods. After an initial defeat, the official of the king of Aram advised him, "Their gods are gods of the hills. That is why they were too strong for us. But if we fight them on the plains, surely we will be stronger than they."

The next spring, Ben-Hadad mustered a huge army and invaded the land of the Hebrews a second time. Yahweh, the God of Israel, was incensed. Through an unnamed prophet, he reassured Ahab, "Because the Arameans think the Lord is a god of the hills and not a god of the valleys, I will deliver this vast army into your hands, and you will know that I am the Lord." It goes without saying that Israel's army won the day, and Ben-Hadad escaped by the skin of his teeth. Yahweh and Israel broke the power of Aram.

Probably the best known passage about "territorial spirits" is Daniel 10. Daniel had been praying for revelation and for the deliverance of his exiled people, Israel. In a delayed response, a great angel, Michael, finally reached Daniel with God's answer. "Do not be afraid, Daniel," Michael exclaimed. "Since the first day you set your mind to gain understanding and to humble yourself before your God, your words were heard, and I have come in response to them. *But the prince of the Persian kingdom resisted me twenty-one days*" (Dn 10:12ff, italics mine).

John Calvin wrote of this passage, "When Daniel introduces the angel of the Persians and the angel of the Greeks, he undoubtedly intimates that certain angels are appointed as a kind of precedence over kingdoms and providences."[19]

"Territorial spirits" is now a popular expression that refers to the hierarchy of dark angels strategically assigned by Satan himself to influence and control nations, communities and even families. A multilevel system of spiritual beings is suggested by Ephesians 6:12: rulers, authorities, the powers of this dark world, the spiritual forces of evil. C. Peter Wagner has concluded that

> Satan delegates high-ranking members of the hierarchy of evil spirits to control nations, regions, cities, tribes, people groups, neighborhoods, and other significant networks of human beings throughout the world. Their major assignment is to prevent God from being glorified in their territory, which they do through directing the lower-ranking demons.[20]

What can we do about this? Sometimes we can be more effective in deliverance ministry when we discern the demons resisting our prayers. Similarly, releasing our families from generational sins and curses can be more readily achieved if we are able to identify the dark angels assigned to torment us. The same thing can be said for the growth and success of a local church, or the advance of the kingdom of God in a city or a nation. Logically, the better you know your enemy, the better chance you have defeating him. To enhance their chance of winning, football teams studiously watch game films of their opponents.

God, I believe, will show us what kind of spiritual powers we are confronting—when we need to know. But a precise knowledge of specific territorial spirits is not the important focus of spiritual warfare. What we really need to know, and the only thing we need to know, is that Jesus is Lord, and we will overcome the devil and his dark angels through the blood of the Lamb and the word of our testimony (Rv 12:11).

Clinton Arnold, professor of theology at Talbot Theological Seminary in California and a fresh voice in the spiritual warfare movement, has done extensive research on principalities and powers in Paul's letter to the Ephesians. Arnold points out that "while Paul has much to say about the powers of darkness, there is a lot that he does not say."[21] Specifically, Paul does not address the popular ideas about territories ruled by evil angels. Arnold cautions us,

> Although Paul showed a great deal of dependence on the book of Daniel for some of his terms and concepts... Paul himself never connected the powers of darkness with any specific country or territory. For instance, he never entreated God to thwart the angelic prince over Rome or to bind the demonic ruler over Corinth.... What Paul stressed is the recognition that there are powerful demonic emissaries who attack the church and hinder its mission and that they can be overcome only through reliance on the power of God.[22]

I believe there are territorial spirits, area-bound angels. Angels seem to be assigned to specific geographical regions, but let's walk through this new "territory" cautiously. My wariness about this issue is related to a point I've been hammering on all through this book: *Christian believers—and students, and writers, and scholars—must remain unwaveringly biblical.* There are a lot of things we have to talk about. And think about. And write about. And pray about.

But we have to keep coming back to the Bible, like the early

Christians in Berea, who were of more noble character than other Christians. What a value judgment! Why? Because "they received the message with great eagerness." They weren't religious blockheads, closed to any new ideas. And yet they "examined the Scriptures every day to see if what Paul [and everybody else] said was true" (Acts 17:11). Which leads me to one more caution for students of angels, dark and light.

THE DANGER OF DUALISM

Dualism is the belief in two *equally* powerful forces in the universe—Good and Evil. Or one great "Force" which can somehow be manipulated for good or evil. But it isn't true. The philosophy espoused in the Star Wars books and movies is a myth. Clinton Arnold writes, "While Christ and the church are represented throughout the New Testament as being in conflict with the powers, never were these opposing forces free and independent of God's absolute sovereignty. God is sovereign because he is the Creator."[23]

As clear as the Bible is on the reality of our Adversary and his significant power and influence, the Scriptures do not teach "dualism," the idea of two opposing, equally powerful forces in everlasting conflict. The devil may be the second most powerful being in universe, but he runs a distant second to the Triune God who created him.

There are two equal and opposite errors into which our race can fall about the devils. One is to disbelieve in their existence. The other is to believe, and to feel an excessive and unhealthy interest in them. They themselves are equally pleased by both errors, and hail a materialist and a magician with the same delight.

C. S. Lewis, The Screwtape Letters

Satan and his dark angels work hard throwing up "smoke screens" to keep us from realizing their limitations. Something happened to me on a family vacation a few years ago that illustrates this point.

Packing our kids and a whole lot of stuff into our family van, we headed out to see America in a three-week family vacation. I had scheduled a whole day-and-a-half to see everything in Washington, D.C., and we ended up spending most of that time visiting the Smithsonian—a favorite destination for tourists from around the world.

The Smithsonian is a vast collection of museums that could take weeks to see, but we hurried through two or three of the most popular. One of our favorites was the Air and Space Museum, which features everything from the original Wright brothers' aircraft to displays of advanced space exploration. Before a major renovation, the Air and Space Museum used to have a life-sized diorama of a World War I airfield command post.

Behind the door of an old, dimly lit shanty, you could hear the scratchy, tape-recorded voice of an angry, blustering officer discussing aerial strategy and his plans for the day. And through the window, on the far wall of the little shack was a hulking, moving shadow, an imposing silhouette of the commander pacing back and forth in nervous concern.

I wonder how they did that? I thought to myself. So I leaned over the anti-tourist barrier and stuck my head through the pane-less window. There on the floor was what looked like a record player with a tiny—maybe six inches high—cardboard figure going round and round in front of a sixty watt light bulb. The imposing silhouette was merely a clever illusion! Nothing was in the building! "Just like the devil!" I whispered.

Without a doubt, there is a devil assisted by a myriad of wicked beings of unquestioned power. But the reality is that *the devil is not as big as he looks*. Satan's power has definite limits, and he has already been defeated: "And having disarmed the powers and authorities, he [Christ] made a public spectacle of them, triumphing over them by the cross" (Col 2:15).

There is a devil. Demons are real. The War of the Ages rages on. Sometimes it even seems like God is powerless and evil will prevail. Just this morning, one of the headlines in our newspaper grieved, "Another bloody day in the Valley: 5 dead, 2 hurt in 4 incidents." In the book of Revelation the souls of the martyrs, brutally murdered in the early persecutions of the church, cried out from under the altar, "How long, Sovereign Lord, holy and true, until you judge the inhabitants of the earth and avenge our blood?" (Rv 6:10)

How long, God? Is God really sovereign? Is he really holy and true? Yes. And how big is the devil? Stick your head in the window and look for yourself. He's just an imposing illusion. In the end, he's not very big at all: "And the devil, who deceived them, was thrown into the lake of burning sulfur, where the beast and the false prophet had been thrown. They will be tormented day and night for ever and ever" (Rv 20:10).

CHAPTER ELEVEN

A New Age of Angels

We must know the truth about the occult and the spirit world to combat erroneous and increasingly popular views. We must recognize the titanic struggle carried on every day between forces of darkness and forces of light.

C. Fred Dickason,
Angels: Elect and Evil

Only in the New Age would it be possible to invent an angel so mellow that it can be ignored.

Nancy Gibbs,
Time, **December, 1993**

Good books on good angels are scarce, although there's a profusion of Christian books on Satan, demons, the occult and spiritual warfare. Meanwhile, beautifully published angel books with a New Age twist are multiplying. I found five in just a few minutes in a local mall bookstore—and what I read troubled me. Angels are taking us by storm, and some of the clouds are very dark.

One New Age writer informs us, by angelic revelation, that "we are currently in the rising of the third great wave of angels... The angels are opening to us as never before. Something profound is on the move. And each one of us, to the precise extent that we can sustain the vision, is part of this great plan."[1]

People are not just writing books about angels, angels are *telling* them to write books. In *Ask Your Angels: A Practical Guide to Working with the Messengers of Heaven to Empower and Enrich Your Life*, Alma Daniel and her co-authors actually asked their "recording angel" for "inside information." Their angel "Abigrael" revealed to them,

> "What I've been commissioned to share with you for this book is how things are now.... Later in this book I will be giving you up-to-the-minute briefings on how [Gabriel, Michael, Raphael, and Uriel] are now working for you. This is not the same as the information you have from the past.... Michael, for example, was always seen with a sword, cutting away evil. But as you are now mastering duality, Michael doesn't need to do that."[2]

This is blatantly deceptive, very much like Satan's temptation of Adam and Eve. Aeons ago the Serpent taunted, "You will not surely die, for God knows that when you eat of the tree your eyes will be opened, and you will be like God, *knowing good and evil*" (Gn 3:4-5, italics mine). Or "mastering duality," as the New Age angel Abigrael puts it. Sounds to me like the angels, at least the seductive ones, haven't changed their tune. The sad thing is that people are still singing along. The ancient, undying deception elevates *knowing* good and evil over *doing* good and *disdaining* evil.

A COMPULSIVE FASCINATION WITH
THE PARANORMAL

The New Age movement is evidence that people are starving for spiritual reality—any kind. Something deep inside tells us that there is a God and, perhaps, a myriad of immortal beings somewhere just beyond time and space. But it's just a hunch. Our spiritual ignorance and vulnerability are the terrible downside of all this. To many people, like the authors of New Age angel books, an angel is an angel is an angel. No distinction is made between good and evil angels.

People, all kinds of people, Christians and non-Christians, have a compulsive fascination with the paranormal: science fiction, UFOs, ghosts, exorcisms, *and angels*. The danger lies in the fact that we have no natural ability to sort through it all. We have an instinctive need to touch the spiritual dimension—but no point of reference to understand it without the Holy Spirit and God's Word.

On the "up" side, our fascination with spiritual phenomena is primitive evidence of the existence of God. In the middle of this century, Dietrich Bonhoeffer wrote theology for what he called "a world come of age." He was living in an era of unprecedented scientific and technical advances, when it seemed like the notion of God was becoming increasingly unnecessary. Karl Marx had said some decades earlier that religion was like a drug, mesmerizing the masses. Now the world was growing up—and growing out of its need for relationship with a divine being. By the early 1960s, God was dead, or so we were told.

Never in his deepest theological moments could Bonhoeffer have foreseen the unprecedented, worldwide surge in religion within just fifty years of his death in 1945. God wouldn't die, because his image is stamped on every human heart. The world is more religious now than ever. "Religious revival of the Third Millennium" is what John Naisbitt and Patricia Aburdene call it in their landmark book, *Megatrends 2000*, which has been read almost religiously by leaders in government, business, and education. Naisbitt and Aburdene have actually pointed to religion as one of the ten most significant socio-cultural trends taking us into the next century. "Religious belief," they announce, "is intensifying worldwide under the gravitational pull of the year 2000."[3]

New technologies and a "new world order" have not lessened our need for God. If anything, people have become desperate for—and vulnerable to—reality beyond the materialism and frenzy of our increasingly godless society. New Ager and angel author Terry Lynn Taylor said recently at the first Angels and Nature Spirit Conference, "Technology is not filling our souls with happiness. People are re-evaluating what this is really about. *The angels*," she writes, "*are helping people have hope*, letting us know there is another force."[4]

Taylor suggests that angels are part of the solution, but that's the problem. People are turning to religion in unprecedented numbers, but it's religion of their own choosing, sometimes of their own making. Not every religious belief is right and not every angel is good. Angels are not just helping people have hope; dark angels in disguise are helping people discover wrong religion. And without the bedrock of the Bible, people can get themselves into deep religious trouble. Angel revelations must be taken very seriously and examined very closely. Angel experiences are wonderful, powerful, and ominous.

ANGELS MAKE YOUR HEAD SPIN

We're kidding ourselves if we think we can match wits with the angels. They're interested in us, for better or for worse, and the less informed we are, the more dangerous dark angels become. In fact, we need to recognize how difficult it is for any of us to interpret spiritual experiences. We are helpless without the help of God, a working knowledge of Scripture, and the counsel of other wise Christians.

Even the Apostle John was momentarily confused by the appearance of an angel. John described himself as the disciple closest to Jesus. He reclined next to the Lord at the Last Supper (Jn 21:20), and as he watched the Savior dying on the cross, he heard Jesus say to his mother Mary, "Dear woman, here is your son." From that time on, we are told, John took the mother of Jesus into his own home (Jn 19:25-27).

Later, near the end of his life, the aging apostle was imprisoned on the little Greek island of Patmos. Exiled and isolated, alone "in the Spirit on the Lord's day," John received the prophecies and visions that became the Book of Revelation. In his opening chapter, John describes a dazzling appearance of the resurrected, glorified Christ. "His head and hair were white like wool, as white as snow, and his eyes were like blazing fire.... His face was like the sun shining in all its brilliance" (Rv 1:14-16). When John saw him, he fell at his feet "as though dead" (Rv 1:17).

The same kind of thing happened at the end of the Book of Revelation. At the conclusion of his visions, John fell down in worship again. But this time it was an angel, who objected, "Do not do it! I am a fellow servant with you and with your brothers the prophets and all who keep the words of this book. Worship God!" (Rv 22:8-9).

Here we have an outstanding example of the power and persuasiveness of real angel experiences. John, an intimate and personal friend of Jesus before his resurrection, the oldest and the last living apostle with years of Christian leadership under his belt, could not distinguish between the glorified Christ at the beginning of his book and the angel at the end. He worshipped them both! How could this possibly happen? Because angels are awesome, and we can be downright defenseless in their presence. If an angel could fool a wise old apostle, what about us?

John fell before the angel in blind, compulsive worship, but the good angel would not allow it. We can learn a couple of very important things from this. First, angels are not to be worshipped under any circumstances. "Thou shalt worship the Lord thy God and him only shalt thou serve." Second, spiritual experiences can be so forceful that they lead us to do things we would never consider doing in a saner frame of mind. But God's good angels *never* mislead us, or take worship for themselves. They always point us back to God.

This simply cannot be said for the fallen angels. What an angel says, does, and allows will give us clues about who he's working for. We must use the truth of the Bible to judge every angelic encounter. Truth overruled by experience is the bear trap of deception. Here's an example:

> The swirling fog began to dissipate, and I could see the flicker of a light ahead—a darting, pulsating glow resembling a fire-fly. I paused for a moment to observe, and the tiny flare expanded in size and appeared as a small full moon touching the earth. As I moved closer to the radiance, it suddenly changed into a vertical beam, a pillar of transparent light.
>
> "Are you the angel I am seeking?" I asked.
>
> The soft yet powerful feminine voice replied, "I am the Angel of Creative Wisdom."
>
> "Do you have a name?"
>
> "Some have called me Isis," she said, and with those words the pillar of light slowly materialized to reveal the face and form of a beautiful woman wearing a flowing white robe trimmed in gold.[5]

What would you do if you had an experience like this? Would you believe it? Would you worship? This encounter, as it is recounted in the opening chapter of *The Angels Within Us*, is as real as the book you are holding in your hand. But it's the wrong side of real. This angel doesn't point anyone to God. She draws all the attention to herself, and what she says betrays her New Age bias: "Know your true nature and hold your mind focused on that highest aspect of your being until it is realized. The more you are infused with the energy of your divine mind, the greater the restoration of the chord of wisdom."[6]

Not everything that glitters is heavenly gold. Not every bright angel is from heaven. The Apostle Paul alerted the early Christians, "Satan himself masquerades *as an angel of light*" (2 Cor

11:14, italics mine). The devil never looks like the devil. If he did, no one would be suckered by his schemes. Sometimes the devil looks just like an angel! He much prefers to appear in "the darting, pulsating glows," "the pillar of transparent light" of "the Angel of Creative Wisdom."

Nearly fifteen hundred years ago, an early Christian writer by the name of Lactantius cautioned in his *Divine Institutes,* "These impure and wandering spirits, that they may throw all things into confusion, and overspread the minds of men with errors, interweave and mingle false things with true."

MORONI AND OTHER DARK ANGELS OF FALSE RELIGIONS

Not every angel is from God. Listen to this blatant denial of evil from a recent New Age publication, and notice especially how this information comes from "angelic informants" (emphasis mine):

> Even in this day and age, films like *The Omen, Rosemary's Baby,* and *The Seventh Sign* evoke horror because they tap into the possibility that we may be influenced in some way by universal messengers of evil. *However, according to our angelic informants,* the situation, thank God, is not like that at all.... Slowly, surely, we are collectively emerging from this *illusion of evil....* Many contemporary Christians have begun to abandon the concept that there is a real devil, recognizing once again that there is only one omnipotent force in the universe.[7]

Angels appear in virtually every religion. If Christianity is true, and there are *not* multiple paths to God, then perhaps angels—dark angels dressed in light—are responsible for the birth of other religions. The apostle Paul's view of the origin of pagan religion was not politically correct: "Do I mean then that a sacrifice offered to an idol is anything, or that an idol is anything?

No, but the sacrifices of pagans *are offered to demons"* (1 Cor 10:19-20, italics mine). The same idea is suggested in the Psalms: "For great is the Lord and most worthy of praise; he is to be feared above all gods. *For all the gods of the nations are idols*, but the Lord made the heavens" (Ps 96:4-5, italics mine).

Mormonism is one of the most stunning examples of the power and influence of dark angels disguised in light. An angel by the name of Moroni appeared to Joseph Smith and told him that the entire church had fallen out of God's favor and could not be salvaged. It was time, Moroni announced, for someone to restart the church. An angel appearance and ongoing angelic encounters are the foundation stones of Mormonism. Listen to Joseph Smith describing Moroni's first appearance, something the Mormons call "the precious angel message":

> I called... upon the Lord and he showed unto me a heavenly vision, for behold an angel of the Lord came and stood before me and... he revealed unto me that in the Town of Manchester, Ontario County, N.Y. there were plates of gold upon which there were engravings which were engraven by Moroni and his fathers, the servants of the living God in ancient days, and deposited by the commandments of God and kept by the power thereof and that I should go and get them..."[8]

A more recent Mormon publication on angels is devoted to proving, more or less, that God has always used angels to teach *new* truth. This is necessary, of course, to undergird the doctrines of Mormonism. The author McConkie explains that, in the very beginning of time "God established a pattern of his teaching men by way of angels. It started with the first man, Adam." McConkie concludes, "Thus, the basic relationship between the Son of God and man was announced and taught by an angel. *This system of teaching has been repeated over and over again*. The Book of Mormon furnishes the best examples of the use of angels as teachers."[9]

Do you catch the irony of his logic? An angel appeared to

Joseph Smith guiding him to start a new religion. Then the angel allegedly leads him to the discovery of sacred, golden tablets, which he translates into the contents of the Book of Mormon, which in turn "furnishes the best of examples of the use of angels as teachers." In other words, the angel who is guiding Joseph Smith gives him new scriptures that "prove" that angels give new scriptures! That's like me telling you, "I'm God," and then leading you to a holy book—which *I* have just written—that "proves" it.

Irrational? Yes, but ultimately, the issues we face confronting false religious beliefs—Mormon or otherwise—are never purely rational. They are forcefully spiritual. Like many New Age writers, Joseph Smith came face to face with an incredibly powerful dark angel, and he had nothing in him to resist. If you corner Mormons with logical contradictions of their doctrinal system, they will invariably fall back on their own personal religious experience, just like the father of their religion—something they call their "testimony," a burning moment of personal revelation that Mormonism is the only true religion. I am persuaded that the burning moment is orchestrated by dark angels dressed in light.

How important are angels to Mormons? The "precious angel message" was plenty powerful to get the movement going, but to keep it going, Mormon teaching has incorporated a system of constant angelic revelation. McConkie continues, "*We are indebted to angels for much or our understanding in gospel scholarship* [that is, in actually understanding scripture]. The Aaronic Priesthood[10] holds the keys to the ministering angels.... Quite literally this means that those who hold the Aaronic Priesthood are in a position to have angels minister unto them... [and] *one is not fully enjoying his office and calling in the absence of such wondrous experiences.*"[11]

Mormon "testimonies" are genuine, but the angels that inspire them are impure. This is why the apostle Paul sternly warned the early church, "I am astonished that you are so quickly deserting the one who called you by the grace of Christ and are turning to a different gospel—which is really no gospel at all. Evidently some people are throwing you into confusion and are trying to pervert the gospel of Christ. But even if we *or an angel from heaven* should preach a gospel other than the one we preached to you, let him be eternally condemned" (Gal 1:6-8, italics mine).

An angel started Mormonism, and angels perpetuate it. Seducing angels, upholding a different gospel, not the Christ of the New Testament, are the mediators and revelators of Mormonism. In striking contrast, Christian theologian Karl Barth observed that angels "are only the servants of God and man.... They are essentially marginal figures. This is their glory." In other words, angels are not in the center of the real Christian gospel. Jesus is.

HOW TO RECOGNIZE SEDUCING ANGELS

How, then, can we distinguish between good and evil angels? A few years ago, J. Rodman Williams, distinguished theologian and author of the new three-volume *Renewal Theology*, convened with several other Christian leaders to respond to "the widespread expression of concern about the book *Angels on Assignment*, by the late Pastor Roland Buck." Basing its cautions on 1 John 4:1, where Christians are commanded "to test the Spirits," and 1 Thessalonians 5:21, where we are told to "test everything," the council recommended five tests of the validity of angelic encounters:

One, are angels identified by non-biblical names? Two, are the angels given an extra-biblical description? Three, are the angels performing roles beyond what the Bible reveals about them? Four, are angels sources of additional information beyond the teaching of the Bible? Five, are the angels in any way proclaiming another gospel, another way to heaven, a "revised" form of Christianity?

Notice how the Bible is the key in each of these tests. Let's look at each of them in more detail.

Test 1. Are angels identified by non-biblical names? Gustav Davidson, author of *A Dictionary of Angels*, has compiled a comprehensive collection of over three hundred pages of specific angel names gathered from a variety of sources, primarily nonbiblical. As we have seen in an earlier chapter, only two angel names appear in the Bible: Michael and Gabriel. Davidson writes, "At first I thought that angels, named angels, were to be found only in the Bible. I soon learned that, on the contrary, the Bible was the last place to look for them."[12]

The Bible is the *last* place to find them? Look out! Are there angels identified by nonbiblical names? In Davidson's book? Hundreds. In the case of Mormonism? Yes. In the case of all the recent New Age books on angels? Yes, many. John Randolf Price, whose angel encounter I cited at the very beginning of this chapter, has selected and named twenty-two qualities or virtues with which he identifies specific angels, like "the angel of creative wisdom," "the angel of abundance," and "the angel of loving relationships."

Price explains, "The universe is a macrocosm of creative energy and power, and every man, woman, and child is the epitome of this totality of the cosmos. Within your individualized energy field, the microcosm called *you*, are twenty-two Causal Powers, or angels, that control your conscious behavior and govern the manifestation of all forms and experiences in your personal life."[13] Price's "angel of loving relationships," we discover at the very end of the book, finds its archetype in Krishna, Master of Heaven, a powerful being in the pantheon of Hindu gods.

What makes books like this so terribly misleading is the mixing of Scripture, Christian beliefs, and general religious and New Age ideas. How does Price introduce us to the Angel of Creative Wisdom? By quoting the Bible! His opening line is from Psalm 91:11: "For he will give his angels charge of you to guard you in all your ways."

But the Angel of Creative Wisdom is not even slightly interested in the Bible. In fact, truth is cleverly and completely abandoned as this dazzling angel repeats, *"Regardless of what your mind tells you, what does your intuition say?"*[14]

Test 2. Are the angels given an extrabiblical description? In other words, what do they look like? Is their appearance like that of angels in the Bible? The Bible not only reveals that angels exist, it also lets us know something about how they look. This is not to say that a person must report his or her angel encounter in strictly biblical terms in order for it to be valid. Remember, when depicting the spiritual realm, we are often at a loss for words, and different people may see and describe things in different ways.

But angelic visions today should have a general relationship to the appearance of angels in Scripture, and when someone describes angels in great and unusual detail, listeners beware. The focus of the Bible is always on the message, not on exactly what the messenger looks like.

To illustrate, J. Rodman Williams uses one of Roland Buck's angel stories:

> No two of them look alike! They are different sizes, have different hairstyles, and completely different appearances. Chrioni [a nonbiblical angel name] has a hairdo much like many men have today, and he looks about twenty-five years old. I do not know what he would weigh in earthly pounds, but my guess would be close to four hundred pounds. He is huge, seven or more feet in height, and often [apparently Buck saw him many times] wears a brown pull-over shirt and is casually, but neatly dressed in loose-fitting brown trousers. His shirt laces at the top with what looks like a shoelace. Gabriel often appears [apparently Buck saw him often, too] in a shimmering white tunic with a radiant gold belt about five inches wide, white trousers and highly polished, bronze-colored shoes.[15]

This fascinating but fanciful angel description goes well beyond the modest, albeit resplendent, appearances of angels in the Bible. Details prove nothing. In fact, too many details may actually prove that the angel seen was not from God, because good angels simply do not bring a lot of attention to themselves. Exact and elaborate descriptions of angels appearing in their nonearthly forms challenge the very essence of angelic encounters in the Bible: those kinds of manifestations are indescribable.

Test 3. Are the angels performing roles beyond what the Bible reveals about them? In Terry Lynn Taylor's angel book with a New Age twist, *Guardians of Hope: The Angel Guide to Personal Growth*, angels are, among other things, mediators and guardians of Twelve Step recovery programs! In one section called "Practice One: Your inner wise angel guide," she writes,

> Angels can help us understand what intuition means in a personal way. Angels are actually in charge of a large part of our intuitive self. Viewing intuition from the perspective of angel consciousness, we can say that intuition is our way of tapping into a higher power for guidance and awareness.... For this practice, go into angel alpha state and begin to imagine your wise and inner guide.... [T]ry to get past the need to define. [Don't think about the truth!] As you go deeper into angel alpha, begin to feel at one with the light, a oneness with all creation in this timeless place where you are free from the heaviness of earth and your body. Imagine you are meeting your wise angel guide.[16]

Spiritual experiences like this are genuinely real, but the angels of Taylor's book are doing extrabiblical things.

Test 4: Are angels sources of additional information beyond the teaching of the Bible? There is no better example of this than the *Book of Mormon*, to which Mormons refer fondly as "scripture," so high is their regard for what "the angel" revealed to Joseph Smith.[17] Paul wrote, "But even if we or an angel from heaven should preach a gospel other than the one we preached to you, let him be eternally condemned" (Gal 1:8).[17]

Test 5. Are the angels in any way proclaiming another gospel, another way to heaven, a "revised" form of Christianity? If you ask this question of Mormonism, for example, you get an unequivocal *yes.* If you ask the question about New Age books on angels, the answer is again *yes.*

Roland Buck makes the outrageous observation, "One thing God told me was... opposite to my theology... I have preached that once you quit breathing, if you are not saved, and do not know God, you have missed heaven. God said that was not necessarily so. He said that there is a spot where the spirit of mankind may linger for a little time before going to their permanent abode."

Buck receives this information from an even higher authority than Gabriel or Michael, presumably from God himself. But his words, as comforting as they may seem, contradict God's Word about what happens to people when they die: the righteous proceed into the presence of God; the ungodly go straight to hades. What Roland Buck reports simply does not stand up to the fifth test.

In contrast, genuine experiences with good angels will always survive careful biblical analysis. An example is a story given to me by my friend Cheryl Sacks.

It was 1977. I was living in the Dallas, Texas, area, where I was teaching high school English. I had just moved into a new apartment and my new bedroom furniture had not yet arrived. I was spending my nights on a mattress on my bedroom floor.

One morning I was awakened early by a loud rustling noise. It seemed like the sound was right next to my ear. My first thought was that someone near me was crumpling tissue paper, but when I tried to open my eyes, the light in my room was so bright I simply could not get them open. My struggle to open my eyes lasted for what seemed like several minutes.

Finally, managing a feeble squint, I saw a huge angelic being standing beside me. The first thing I remember seeing was the wings, and I realized that's what was causing the rustling sound I had heard moments before. I was awestruck by both the beauty and whiteness of the wings. I had never seen anything so lovely. Both the wings and the clothing of the angel were a brilliant white; it was white unlike any earthly white I have ever seen.

The angel was huge and seemed to touch the ceiling, but I was not sure. I looked up, up, up, but because of the brilliance radiating from the angel, I was never able to see his face. In fact, I had to stop looking. I just couldn't keep my eyes open.

For the next several days I felt the tangible anointing or presence of the Lord all over my body.

Cheryl's experience is parallel with angel encounters in the Bible. Let's use the five tests to evaluate what Cheryl claims to have experienced:

Test 1: Are angels identified by non-biblical names? In Cheryl's story? No!

Test 2: Are the angels given an extrabiblical description? In Cheryl's story? No. She saw an angel, no doubt, but her description is vague, general, lacking details. And what she tells us about the angel is much like what we find about angels in the Bible. Remember, a highly detailed description of an angel is suspicious.

Test 3: Are the angels performing roles beyond what the Bible reveals about them? In Cheryl's story? No. The angel does nothing unusual. In fact, Cheryl's angel did nothing, period. I asked her why she thought the angel appeared to her, if the angel didn't say or do anything in particular. Asserting that this was her only experience like this ever, she told me that her spiritual life, her walk with God, had been dramatically changed by the angelic encounter. Particularly, she was profoundly reassured of God's love for her and his protection of her life.

Test 4: Are angels sources of additional information beyond the teaching of the Bible? In the case of Cheryl's angel, absolutely not.

Test 5: Are the angels in any way proclaiming another gospel, another way to heaven? Again, in the case of Cheryl's angel, not at all.

With all the current interest in angels and the paranormal, we must be wary. If we are not discerning, or if we are bound by our own sense of religious self-importance—unwilling to be uncompromisingly biblical and relentlessly honest with our-selves— "Abigrael," or "Moroni," or "Chrioni," or "the Serpent," or some other bright phantom spirit will lead us into a religion of darkness and death.

It is absolutely necessary to study and embrace what the Bible tells us about angels. Karl Barth insisted that the "teacher and master to which we must keep in this matter can only be the Holy Scriptures of the Old and New Testament, that we must not accept any other authority, that we must listen exhaustively to what this guide has to tell us, and that we must respect what it says and what it does not say."[18]

CHAPTER TWELVE

In the Line of Fire

Few people realize the profound part angelic forces play in human events. **Billy Graham**

For our struggle is not against flesh and blood, but against... the powers of this dark world and against the spiritual forces of evil in the heavenly realm.

Ephesians 6:12

I understood spiritual warfare, but I hadn't really experienced it. Until 1987. It was the worst of years. I was serving as the pastor of a large and growing church, and everything was going as well as I could imagine. I had even said to my wife in the summer of 1986 how wonderfully life was treating us. I remember sitting at our breakfast table, the warm sunlight washing through the bay windows, and talking about how happy I was. And that I probably ought to enjoy it, because one never knows when things will change.

And did things ever change! Unknown to me, there were little problems in our church that would breed like a disease in stagnant water on a hot summer day. Within six months, my summer of happiness became a winter of discontent, followed by a spring and summer of confusion and depression. And an autumn of death.

I had no idea how badly Christian friends and associates could hurt each other. It was a story with a familiar ring for those who have been in Christian work for any length of time: misunderstanding, broken relationships, and hurt and pain for everyone involved. I can't say I have ever seriously considered taking my own life, but I had moments in the late spring of 1987 when my depression was so severe that I thought to myself, "I am feeling the kind of despair that people feel when they commit suicide. Now I understand why people can't bear to see their life go on." Members of my immediate family thought I was losing my mind.

But the year wasn't over. In October, after feeling an intense pressure in my chest for months, my heart suddenly stopped beating regularly—to the tune of about ten thousand misfires a day. My cardiologist, recognized as one of the best diagnosticians in the Southwest, decided after many tests that I had a mild case of cardiomyopathy—a mysterious weakening of the heart. The only cure for cardiomyopathy, I found out later, is a heart transplant.

And then people at the church started having terrible accidents. In November, my senior associate's wife came within inches of death in a serious automobile accident on her way home from church! Two miles from the church, she collided with a pickup, driven by someone else from our congregation—*on his way to church!*

A few days after Christmas, our receptionist's husband was killed in a single-car highway accident, and our beloved visitation pastor, Warren Hill, died of cancer. I conducted back-to-back funerals the last two days of 1987.

It was spiritual warfare of the worst kind. It was like a miniature of Revelation 9:1-3:

> And I saw a star that had fallen from sky to the earth. The star [Satan] was given the key to the shaft of the Abyss. When he opened the Abyss, smoke rose from it like the smoke from a gigantic furnace. The sun and sky were darkened by the smoke from the Abyss [which turned out to be]... locusts... given power like that of scorpions....

There were times during that year when great clouds of darkness, it seemed, were smothering the life of God in our church offices and in my home. I can only conclude that a singularly powerful dark angel, "a ruler of the darkness," had been commissioned to destroy us.

1987 was the best of years, as well. Six years later, I'm still alive! Our church miraculously survived the crisis to become one of the two hundred fastest-growing churches in America.[1] And my heart is just fine. I have subsequently seen a different cardiologist, who has given me a different diagnosis—"a benign arrythmia." "Benign" is one of the best words in medical terminology. And I have developed a profound understanding of how powerful spiritual forces shape the circumstances of our lives.

Angels are real. Demons are real. Life is a real spiritual battle. Once there was a "war in heaven." The Bible says that, "Michael *and his angels* fought against the dragon, and the dragon *and his angels* fought back.... The great dragon was hurled down—that ancient Serpent called the devil, or Satan.... *He was hurled to the earth, and his angels with him*" (Rv 12:7-9, italics mine).

And that's the problem. Our struggle now, here on the earth, "is *not* against flesh and blood, but... against the spiritual forces of evil in the heavenly realms" (Eph 6:12).

Up to this point in the book, I have been unfolding the doctrines of angels and devils, trying to help you understand what the Bible teaches us about the spiritual dimension. I've shared with you many angel reports, and I've interjected insights and warnings about dark angels. But a book about angels dark and light would not be complete without a look at the big picture. In other words, every one of us needs to understand how angels and demons fit into the larger scheme of things, into God's timeless purposes for his creation.

THE BIG PICTURE

Have you ever assembled a jigsaw puzzle? We've done a few on lazy summer vacation evenings. Some puzzles are unmercifully intricate, but even the simpler ones are next to impossible to assemble without the picture on the box lid. The carton cover is the "big picture" we use to get an overview of where the individual parts fit together in relation to the whole.

The Bible is like a jigsaw puzzle, with tens of thousands of pieces—we call them verses—that together form the picture of God's eternal plan. The big picture on the box lid, *the main theme of the Bible*, is the kingdom of God.

In a recent analysis of ten significant trends facing the church today, best-selling author Howard Snyder believes that one big change will be the church moving from narrow, institutional traditions into a global, kingdom theology.

"In the past decade," he writes, "Christian thinkers in various parts of the world have turned to the biblical theme of the sovereign rule of God as the basic model for Christian theology in the global city."[2]

The kingdom of God is such a key theme in the Bible that Christian writer Richard Lovelace asserts, "The Messianic kingdom is not only the main theme of Jesus's preaching; it is the central category unifying biblical revelation."[3] In other words, the kingdom theme is what ties it all together.

Another Christian writer, John Bright, believes that "the concept of the kingdom of God involves, in a real sense, the total message of the Bible."[4]

Ron Boehme, a leader in the huge missions organization

Youth With A Mission (YWAM), echoes these beliefs in his book *Leadership for the 21st Century:* "The primary message of Christendom is that the King has come and his Kingdom is now being established among all the peoples of the earth. The Kingdom and its King are the center of reality.... The Kingdom of God is the central message of the Bible."[5] Boehme quotes the great preacher, Dr. E. Stanley Jones:

> ... if you have the key to the Kingdom, you find it a master-key, the key to life now and hereafter, life individual and collective.... So for the church to be relevant the answer is simple: Discover the Kingdom, surrender to the Kingdom, make the Kingdom your life loyalty and your life program.[6]

The big picture—the main theme of the Bible—is the kingdom of God. Simply defined, *the kingdom of God is his rule over everything he has made.* Also, the kingdom is now only partly revealed, but will be manifested fully when Jesus comes again. Jesus put it simply as he taught us to pray, *"Thy kingdom come. Thy will be done on earth* as it is in heaven." God wants to get as much of himself and his way of doing things into our world, and he has chosen to do it through us. Jesus said, "You are the salt of the earth.... You are the light of the world" (Mt 5:13-14).

A QUESTION OF DOMINION

The message of the Bible, then, is the account of God's kingdom. All of the pieces of the puzzle, including all the angels dark and light, somehow fit into this grand scheme. Starting in the first chapter of the Bible, God's first order of business for Adam and Eve was for them to rule over all the earth, to have dominion,[7] something the Serpent contested almost immediately.

The devil's purpose was not merely to tempt the first couple to do something bad, but to overthrow the newly established system of God's authority in the earth—human beings. Satan was not, if he could help it, going to let Adam and Eve "have dominion." He wanted it all for himself, which as we saw in an earlier chapter was the cause of his original downfall.

Everyone knows the story—and has suffered as a result. Adam and Eve sinned, but out of their disgraceful failure springs the resurrection of God's original purpose for humankind: to have dominion in the earth. God promised that one day the seed of the woman—a prophetic reference to Christ, whom the New Testament refers to as the "last Adam" (1 Cor 15:45)— would come and crush the head of the Serpent (Gn 3:15). Satan's influence in the earth would be overthrown and God's kingdom would be established.

The rest of the Bible, then, is (1) the history of the people of God, Israel, serving as the forebears of that "seed"; (2) a promise of how the Seed, the Messiah, the Christ ultimately disarms the powers of hell, "triumphing over them by the cross" (Col 2:15); and (3) a guide describing how the church must carry on the mission.

In a blurry replay of the Garden of Eden—this time it's in the wilderness—the Serpent tried his same tricks on the Son of God. His goal? To bring down the Last Adam the same way he brought down the first Adam, by distorting God's Word and trying to get Jesus to doubt what God said and disobey him.

The devil led Jesus up to a high place "and showed him in an instant *all the kingdoms* of the world." He said to him, probably with great composure, "I will give you *all their authority* and splendor... *if* you worship me" (Lk 4:5-7, italics mine). Jesus didn't bend or break. He rebuked the Great Dark Angel, "Worship the Lord your God and serve him only."

Jesus refused to confront the devil on the devil's terms, but three years later took on the devil on God's terms—the cross— and seized kingdom authority. "*All authority in heaven and in the earth,*" Jesus proclaimed after his resurrection, "has been given to me" (Mt 28:18). But not by the devil who had made the sly offer earlier! The heavenly Father exalted the Son over every name that's named and gave him the keys to hell and death. The kingdom authority of God was reestablished in the earth through the beachhead of Calvary.

Christ's supreme sacrifice on the cross both demonstrated his unfathomable love and yielded his ultimate success. Because of this, Paul was able to write in Romans 8, "In all these things we are more than conquerors through him who loved us."

"For I am convinced," Paul continues, "that neither death nor life, *neither angels or demons... nor any powers...* nor anything else in all creation, will be able to separate us from the love of God that is in Christ Jesus our Lord" (Rom 8:37-39, italics mine).

The kingdom of God is a primary theme of the Bible, and Jesus is the King. He is Lord. When God raised him from the dead, he "seated him at his right hand in the heavenly realms, far above all rule and authority, power and dominion" in heaven and in earth (Eph 1:20-21).

BRINGING THE KINGDOM OF GOD TO EARTH

Though Satan has been conquered and sentenced, his judgment is pending and the war rages on. Angels light and dark are the spiritual armies of the kingdoms of heaven and hell. And you and I are in the middle of all this. God has placed everything under Christ's feet—the head of the Serpent included— "and appointed him to be head over everything *for the church which is his body, the fullness of him who fills everything in every way*" (Eph 1:22-23, italics mine). God has chosen to express and demonstrate his kingdom authority *through the church*, as Paul adds, "[God's] intent was that now, through the church, the manifold wisdom of God should be made known to the rulers and authorities [the dark angels] in the heavenly realms" (Eph 3:10).

This was "according to his eternal purpose." In other words, God had the church—and its mission—in mind from the very beginning. We are in the middle of a great cosmic drama, acting out God's purposes in front of an audience of angels, dark and light. This was "according to his eternal purpose," Paul continues, "which he accomplished in Christ Jesus our Lord," the Last Adam. God *didn't* accomplish this through the first Adam. Through the advance of the church, God takes back his territory Earth from the devil.

I have a destiny. I'm not just here to survive. And I'm certainly not here just for my sake. I'm part of a very "big picture." How I understand my role, how my piece fits into the big picture—along with God's eternal purposes—is of utmost importance. The great nineteenth-century revivalist Charles Finney wrote passionately,

> Now the great business of the church is to reform the world—to put away every kind of sin.... The Christian church was designed to make aggressive movements in every direction—to lift up her voice and put forth her energies in high and low places—to reform individuals, communities and governments, and never rest until *the Kingdom and the greatness of the Kingdom* under the whole heaven shall be given to the saints of the Most High God—until every form of iniquity shall be driven from the earth.[8]

We know who wins in the end: "The kingdom of the world has become the kingdom of our Lord and of his Christ, and he will reign for ever and ever!" (Rv 11:15)

It's only from the perspective of the kingdom—"the big picture"—that you will discover:

- the highest purposes of God
- the reason for spiritual warfare
- the role of angels and demons
- your role in the middle of all this

In other words, everything I've written in the previous chapters of this book will not be *fully* understood without the big picture. Angels and demons are not just fascinating footnotes in the study of Christian doctrine. Everything has to fit together.

There is a war going on all around us, and we're not just watching. *Christians are active participants with the angels of light in advancing the kingdom purposes of God in the earth.* And the devil and his dark angels *will* resist us. Sometimes with subtle temptations to sin. Sometimes with clever deceptions. Sometimes with ferocious power and hate.

But in Christ we are more than conquerors, and the holy angels stand by to protect us and to wage war with us. In the final chapter I will share with you some thoughts and strategies on how to "entertain" angels of light—and how to defend yourself against the angels of darkness.

CHAPTER THIRTEEN

Welcoming the Light, Withstanding the Darkness

Our certainty that angels right now witness how we are walking through life should mightily influence the decisions we make. God is watching, and His angels are interested spectators too. **Billy Graham**

If then we have Angels, let us be sober, as though we were in the presence of tutors; for there is a demon present also. **Chrysostom**

If angels guard us, they have to watch us to guard us. Paul wrote in 1 Corinthians 4:9, "For it seems to me that God has put us apostles on display at the end of the procession, like men con-

197

demned to die in the arena. We have been made a spectacle to the whole universe, *to angels as well as to men*" (italics mine).

Billy Graham tells us in his best-selling book on angels that this verse alludes to the first-century arenas of death, where crowds of vulgar spectators went to see animals killed for sport, men battling to the death and, later, Christians torn apart by lions. In other words, Paul is suggesting here that this world is one vast stadium, one great stage, and all of us are participants in the drama of redemption and righteousness.

We are all being watched closely, but not passively. One author noted, "I have no dramatic encounter to relate of any angelic vision. Yet all through my life, from my first memories, which are very early and very vivid... I have been aware of direction coming to me from a source beyond myself."[1]

There's hardly a human being who does not feel that way. Life is not, as Marx and Darwin wanted us to believe, a chance sequence of unrelated events. Something is nudging me—each of us—to the right or to the left, sometimes preventing me from moving forward, often shoving me from behind. God "guides me in the paths of righteousness" (Ps 23:3), and his holy angels assist in the process. When God lifts his protective hand, we are at the mercy of dark angels. And they have no mercy.

WELCOMING THE ANGELS

The book of Judges records one of the darkest eras in Hebrew history. The Jews were without a central government, and God had withdrawn his covering, leaving the people of Israel wide open to the attacks of the powers of hell. "The angel of the Lord," we are told, "went from Gilgal to Bokim ['a place of weeping'] and said, 'I brought you up out of Egypt and led you into the land that I swore to give to your forefathers.'" The angel of the Lord appeared to announce his displeasure over the way the Hebrews had mismanaged the conquest of Canaan, particularly their failure to destroy completely the inhabitants of the lands around them.

Notice how the angel "brought them out" and "led them." His role was not passive. But because Israel disobeyed—in this case, they made covenants with the Canaanites and did not destroy the heathen altars—the angel of the Lord proclaimed, "Now therefore I tell you that I will not drive them [your enemies] out before you; they will be thorns in your sides *and their gods* [dark angels in the disguise of godlike beings] will be a snare to you" (Jgs 2:1-3, italics mine).

Angels do not watch over us passively. They are actively influencing our lives, both for good and evil. And their activities, as we can see clearly in this Bible text, are directly related to how we live. Look at it again: "Yet you have disobeyed me," the angel retorted. "Why have you done this? Now *therefore...* they will be thorns in your sides."

Life is dangerous. Life is a spiritual battle. And most of the time, it seems, we don't think about how we might be under the influence of dark angels—how the devil is manipulating us toward our destruction. David wrote in Psalm 27, "Teach me your way, O Lord; lead me in a straight path." Why? *"Because of my oppressors.* Do not turn me over to the desire of my foes" (Ps 27: 11-12, italics mine). It really is important to walk the straight and narrow, not just because you're sure to go to hell if you don't, but because hell is sure to come knocking at your door.

In Psalm 34:7 we read that "the angel of the Lord encamps around those *who fear him*, and he delivers them" (italics mine). Don't ignore the condition! Fearing God invites his presence and the angels who accompany him. Not fearing God does just the opposite. Paul challenged the young Timothy, "I charge you, in the sight of God and Christ Jesus *and the elect angels*, to keep these instructions.... " To walk the straight and narrow, because somebody is watching.

This is probably at the heart of what Paul is talking about in a hotly debated text of Scripture, 1 Corinthians 11:5-10, which reads,

And every woman who prays or prophesies with her head uncovered dishonors her head—it is just as though her head were shaved. If a woman does not cover her head, she should have her hair cut off; and if it is a disgrace for a woman to have her hair cut or shaved off, she should cover her head.... For this reason, *and because of the angels*, the woman ought to have a sign of authority on her head (italics mine).

Without getting entangled in the highly charged gender issues here, or how long a woman's hair should be,[2] the overriding message in this Bible passage is that our behaviors are scrutinized by the angels. Gordon Fee, in his widely acclaimed commentary on 1 Corinthians, points out that earlier in Paul's letter (1 Corinthians 4:9), "angels are understood as part of the 'whole universe' before whom Paul's Christian life is on display. Some have therefore argued that the angels were present at the Christian assembly as 'watchers of the created order,'"[3] that is, of the relationships and interactions between men and women.

What Paul wrote here about watching angels may also have some connection with what was taught in the ancient Jewish religious community at Qumran, that angels participate in and assist with public worship.[4] Theologian Henry Theissen concluded that this verse means "the good angels watch all human affairs with deep interest, and... they would be pained to see any infraction of the laws of modesty."[5]

Angels are not just watching *over* us. They're watching us, period! Watching you read this book about them. In some ways, this may be even more unnerving than knowing that God is watching. We're kind of used to God. But multiple heavenly beings? Watching me pray? Watching me eat? Watching me curse at my sputtering lawn mower on a blazing hot Arizona summer day?

My point is this: we wouldn't do a lot of the things we do if our mother was watching. If our sister-in-law was watching. If the pastor was watching. But we forget. Angels dark and light are watching all the time. St. Hilary wrote, "When we are overcome by some evil will, should we not tremble before the presence of the choirs of angels that surround us?"[6] Certainly, an obsessive awareness of omnipresent spirit beings would be just plain unhealthy. And fortunately, angels, for the most part, stay well hidden. But, perhaps, if the spirit realm were more real to us, it might just keep us walking closer to God. It might just help us do a few less regrettable things.

In summary, then, *the angels of light come to our aid when we are believing and obey God, and the dark angels come to oppress us when we don't.* Thus Catholic writer Jean Danielou observed, "Man finds himself in the middle of a spiritual combat between the powers of light and the powers of darkness."[7] And Gregory of Nyssa wrote, "Our human weakness is protected by the assistance of the angels and... in all our perils, provided faith remain with us, we are defended by the aid of spiritual powers."

The spiritual dimension is real, and you and I have the capacity to invite the powers of the invisible realm into our life and experience.

What you do, good or evil, welcomes angelic participation in your life—for good or evil. We already met New Age angels in a previous chapter, but let's revisit them for a moment. Angels, as we have seen, are more popular than ever. Just yesterday, my weekly copy of *Time* magazine arrived in the mail. The cover story: "The New Age of Angels."[8]

Talking with angels has become increasingly fashionable. Deliberately welcoming them into your life. Asking them to speak to you, to work on your behalf. I have already mentioned a recent, best-selling book entitled *Ask Your Angels*. It is, as the subtitle lures us, "a practical guide to working with the messengers of heaven to empower and enrich your lives." I have already pointed out that the Bible nowhere suggests that we are to be "working with the messengers of heaven," although they certainly work with us.

Yet the authors of this very New Age book[9] write enticingly, "People in our workshops are amazed at how easy it is to talk with their angels."[10] And once you've tuned into the angels, the authors add, "you may find yourself receiving other stations as well—voices of guides, extraterrestrials [there are those UFO crews again!], and nature spirits."[11]

I am absolutely convinced that these authors are talking about real encounters with real spirit beings. They aren't making it up. What they describe in captivating detail is really happening to them and their readers. The spiritual dimension is real, and you and I have the capacity to invite the powers of the invisible realm into our life and experience.

But to do so deliberately is dangerous stuff. Religious experience without truth is like a car without a steering wheel. You have no control over where the experience is taking you, and you'll probably end up crashing.

Most people, however, have not gone this far. Striking up a conversation with an angel is not a common experience. Most of our entanglement with dark angels is much more subtle. It has to do, as I have already suggested in this chapter, with our thoughts and behaviors. In fact, I think the devil prefers it this way. His work is, for the most part, indirect and underhanded— but just as powerful as when he appears as an angel-like being. This is why we need to be wise about the underlying forces that shape our lives.

THE ARMOR OF GOD: WITHSTANDING THE DARKNESS

The well-known passage about the armor of God in Ephesians 6 tells us how to resist the more cunning advances of dark angels, and it does this two ways: *directly*, by telling us what we need to do to resist the devil's advances, and *indirectly*, by telling us what areas of our life are vulnerable to the attacks of dark angels. In other words, we not only need the armor, we need to know why we need the armor. Every soldier in training is not only issued the proper equipment and taught how to use it, he is also taught why it's necessary.

We can begin to expose the devil's schemes by asking ourselves why this or that piece of armor is necessary. In other words, if we understand *why* each piece of armor is important, we will recognize the specific avenues that dark angels use to drive into our hearts. Paul writes:

> Our struggle is not with flesh and blood, but against... the powers of this dark world and against the spiritual forces of evil in the heavenly realms. Therefore put on the full armor of God, so that when the day of evil comes, you may be able to stand your ground, and after you have done everything, to stand. Stand firm then, with **the belt of truth** buckled around your waist, with **the breastplate of righteousness** in place, and with **your feet fitted with the readiness... of peace**. In addition to all this, take up **the shield of faith**, with which you can extinguish all the flaming arrows of the evil one. Take **the helmet of salvation** and the sword of the spirit, which is the word of God.   Ephesians 6:12-16 (bold mine)

The belt of truth. The belt of truth is the first of six elements of armor in Ephesians 6. What is it? We should probably begin by talking about what it *isn't*. The belt of truth in this context is not the truth of doctrine or creed. That comes later, when Paul tells us to take up the sword of the Spirit, which is the Word of God. The sword of the spirit is an *offensive* weapon—the power of God's anointed Word spoken in confident faith.

The belt of truth, on the other hand, refers to what's going on in your private life—truth guarding your private parts. The King James almost sounds vulgar: "Gird up your loins with truth." The classic commentary *Expositor's Greek Testament* defines the belt of truth as "the personal grace of *candor, sincerity, truthfulness....* the mind that will practice no deceits and attempt no disguises"[12] What does this tell us indirectly about the dark angels? They specialize in pretense and masquerade, so if you are not sincere, or truthful, or honest with yourself, you may welcome evil spirits into your life.

Satan is the father of lies. It's only logical to conclude, then, that the more you live a lie, the more Satan's power will grip your soul.

This happened to Ananias and Sapphira. Early in the history of the church, as it's recorded in the book of Acts, people were selling all they had to help the work of the ministry and one another. Ananias and his wife Sapphira did the same. *Almost.* They sold what they had and gave *almost* all of it to the apostles. No problem with that, but they gave the impression—*it was a pretense*—that they were giving everything. Listen to Peter's spiritual assessment of what happened: "Ananias, how is it that *Satan has so filled your heart* that you have lied to the Holy Spirit?" (Acts 5:3). Ananias' deceit was an entry point for the dark angel of deceit.

In the best selling book *People of the Lie*, psychiatrist M. Scott Peck writes, "As well as being the Father of Lies, Satan may be said to be a spirit of mental illness. In *The Road Less Travelled* I defined mental health as 'an ongoing process of dedication to reality at all costs.' Satan is utterly dedicated to opposing that process."[13] Twelve Step programs have uncovered the crippling power of self-deceit. They call it *denial.* We have to recognize, then, that our spiritual adversary specializes in lies, and we need to put on the belt of truth as if our life depended on it.

The breastplate of righteousness. What does the breastplate of righteousness tell us about schemes of the devil and dark angels? They are the masters of unrighteousness. Bypassing God's Word—living your life your own way—is a huge risk. Not only is sin self-destructive, it is like a crack in the dam: Bad behaviors release a flood of spiritual oppression. "There is a way," Solomon wrote in Proverbs, "that seems right to a man, but in the end it leads to death" (Prv 14:12).

Paul put it bluntly: "As for you, you were dead in your transgressions and sins, in which you used to live when you followed the ways of this world and of the ruler of the kingdom of the air, the spirit who is now at work in those who are disobedient" (Eph 2:1-2). Paul is telling us here that wickedness is behavior from hell and has terrible consequences, not the least of which is the unhelpful participation of dark forces in your life. And the terrifying thing about this is that those who are influenced to do evil are usually not even slightly aware that they're living "under the influence."

Paul touches on this again in Ephesians 4: "In your anger," he warned, "do not sin. Do not let the sun go down while you are still angry." Why? Because you could "give the devil a foothold." In other words, if we let our anger go unchecked, we risk the chance of exposing ourselves to the direct influence of dark angels. Merrill Unger, the renowned Old Testament scholar, wrote in *Demons in the World Today*, "It is possible for a believer to experience severe demon influence or obsession if he persistently yields to demonic temptation and sin."[14]

So resist the devil and his angels by putting on the breastplate of righteousness, protecting yourself with godliness.

Feet fitted with... the readiness of peace. Jesus declared, "Blessed are the peace*makers*, for they will be called sons of God" (Mt 5:9). Now why would peacemaking qualify us as sons of God? Because God is in the business of making peace. Reconciliation is the theological word for it. "Peace on earth," the angels sang when Christ was born. Paul summed it up: "God was reconciling the world to himself in Christ, not counting men's sins against them. And he has committed to us the message of reconciliation" (2 Cor 5:19).

Sometimes I think this is the area of the devil's greatest success: peace-*breaking*. Peace is elusive. Peace doesn't just happen. You have to work at it. You have to make it happen. Like God did when he sent his Son into the world on a mission of forgiveness and reconciliation. But the world remains full of strife. In the mean streets of dark cities. Between nations. Between races and ethnic groups. Nationalism, as it has been called in the ethnic bloodletting in eastern Europe, is a clever mask for hatred, an intercultural malignancy spread by the devil himself.

It happens in families all the time. Hostility prevails and marriages end, spinning the children into a chasm of confusion, resentment, and shame. And the curse goes on as divorce grips one generation after another. "See to it," the Bible says, "that no bitter root grows up to cause trouble and defile many" (Heb 12:15).

Because our struggle is *not* with flesh and blood but with the underlying divisiveness of dark angels, we should be putting on the shoes of the readiness of peace. Wherever the path of life takes us, we should be ready to make peace, not war. Strife and division, the things that erode relationships, seem to occur naturally—because of the prominence of human selfishness and sin.

You really don't have to look for a fight. One will come your way uninvited sooner or later. Jesus said, "Things that cause people to sin are bound to come, but woe to the person through whom they come" (Lk 17:1). But Paul counters, "Let us therefore *make every effort* to do what leads to peace and to mutual edification" (Rom 14:19, italics mine). Again, peace happens because someone makes it happen. If our heart is filled with God, we will be a ready antidote for the poison of misunderstanding. We will be standing in readiness, the readiness of peace. And we'll thoroughly frustrate the dark angels with the potency of peacemaking.

The shield of faith. It's easy to spot the devil's scheme here. The opposite of faith is doubt and, in its more deliberate form, unbelief. Everybody has doubts. Doubts about ourselves. Doubts about the future. Doubts about God. But when doubt becomes unbelief, life-sustaining faith evaporates. Unbelief is the vacuum of debilitating uncertainty. The skeptic becomes an atheist.

The time when our faith is tested the most, of course, is when everything is going wrong. In the armor of God passage in

Ephesians 6, Paul refers to this as "the day of evil." Maybe this is what the mystics called "the dark night of the soul." The psalmist ended one of his saddest songs, "The darkness is my closest friend" (Ps 88:18). And in Psalm 4, David cautioned, "Be angry, but stand in awe and sin not; commune with your own heart upon your bed" (Ps 4:4, AMPLIFIED).

Paul quotes this verse in Ephesians 4:26, but it's instructive for us to go back to the original Hebrew text of this Psalm. *The Amplified Bible* brings out the richer meaning: "Stand in awe," or "Be deeply moved, and don't sin." In other words, when you're under the surgeon's knife—when you have the greatest reason to move—hold as still as you can!

Trouble moves us deeply. It stirs up our deepest feelings and exposes our greatest weaknesses. Unfortunately, it is when we are in trouble that we are the most vulnerable emotionally and spiritually. We need to hold still, to stay steady at all costs. I like the way J. B. Phillips translates Ephesians 6:13: "Therefore you must wear the whole armor of God that you may be able to resist evil in its day of power, and that even when you have fought to a standstill, you may still stand your ground. Take your stand then...." When everything's at a standstill, stand still!

The greatest test of our faith is under the rain of fire, "the flaming arrows of the wicked one." When the dark angels turn up the heat, everything in us screams, "Turn and run." But Peter reassures us, "Dear friends, do not be surprised at the painful trial you are suffering, as though something strange were happening" (1 Pt 4:12). Why? James explains, "Because you know that the testing of your faith develops perseverance. Perseverance must finish its work so that you may be mature and complete, not lacking anything" (Jas 1:3-4).

I am inclined to believe, therefore, that "the shield of faith" refers more to long-term "faithfulness" than to outbursts of the gift of faith to receive immediate and extraordinary answers to prayer. The shield of faith is faith that endures, faith that fights its way through the feelings of discouragement and failure. Tenacity. Perseverance. The shield of faithfulness.

The helmet of salvation. Your mind is the final line of defense against the influence of dark angels. Dark angels may be the most successful at peace-breaking, but they are the most subtle in their influence of our thoughts. Now rest assured that most of your thoughts are your thoughts—and no matter what you're thinking, you are responsible for those thoughts. But dark angels can influence your thoughts, even though they may not know what you are thinking.

I need to protect my head, then, with the helmet of salvation, because my thought life is such a fierce battleground. Paul wrote in his second letter to the Corinthians,

> For though we live in the world, we do not wage war as the world does. The weapons we fight with are not the weapons of the world. On the contrary, they have divine power to demolish strongholds. We demolish arguments and every pretention that sets itself up against the knowledge of God, *and we take captive every thought to make it obedient to Christ.*
>
> 2 Corinthians 10:3-5 (italics mine)

CAN DARK ANGELS READ MY MIND?

No. But they can surely influence my thoughts. In my book *Overcoming the Dominion of Darkness*, which has an extended section on the armor of God, I wrote that "the longer I serve in ministry and the more I study spiritual warfare, the more I have become convinced that *our thoughts are often influenced by demons.* Not only do we need the helmet of salvation in the sense that our minds need to be saved from old patterns of thinking, but also for guarding our minds against the invasion of demonic influence."[15]

Perhaps the best biblical example is the familiar dialogue between Jesus and Peter in Matthew 16. Jesus was asking his disciples what they were hearing behind his back. "What are people saying about me?" he quizzed them.

"Some say you're John the Baptist; others say Elijah; and still others, Jeremiah or one of the prophets," they responded.

"But what do *you* say about me?" Jesus pressed them. "Who do *you* say that I am?"

Ever-compulsive Peter had a thought pop into his mind: "You are the Christ, the Son of the living God!"

Listen carefully to what Jesus said in reply: "Blessed are you, Simon son of Jonah, *for this was not revealed to you by man, but by my Father in heaven*" (Mt 16:17, italics mine).

Where did Peter's thought come from? The voice of the Father spoke, and Peter "heard" it in his thoughts, but he didn't know that. Peter had no idea that his thinking was being influenced by the spirit realm.

A few verses later, Jesus began to share with his disciples about his impending death. In a rash reversal of spirit, Peter had another thought pop into his mind: "Never, Lord!" he protested. "This will never happen to you!"

Listen again to how Jesus responds. He turned to Peter—and we get the feeling he turned quickly—and roared, "Get behind me, Satan! You are a stumbling block to me."

Who's he talking to? Peter? Or the devil? Or maybe both?

Whatever, it seems quite clear that Peter's newest thought was also originating outside of himself, that somehow the devil himself was intruding into his mind.

As we saw earlier in the chapter, Peter's response to Ananias' deceit is another example of this dynamic of mind and spirit. The same Peter, years later in a more mature and discerning moment, rebuked Ananias, "How is it that Satan has so filled your heart that you have lied to the Holy Spirit?" (Acts 5:3). Most of our thoughts are self-initiated. In other words I think mostly my own thoughts. But sometimes my thoughts originate outside my mind when, like Peter, God himself speaks into my mind and heart. Other times, there's an evil mix, an unconscious partnership with hell. My thoughts are "slimed" by the subtle influence of dark angels.

James wrote about thoughts from heaven and thoughts from hell:

Who is wise and understanding among you? Let him show it by his good life, by deeds done in the humility that comes from wisdom. But if you harbor bitter envy and selfish ambition in your hearts, do not boast about it or deny the truth. *Such "wisdom"* [thoughts, ideas] *does not come down from heaven but is earthly, unspiritual, of the devil.*

James 3:13-15 (italics mine)

Those who deny this influence have no inkling of what's really happening in the spirit world, and therein lies its power and control. Paul believed that "the god of this age *has blinded the minds of unbelievers,* so that they cannot see the light of the gospel of the glory of Christ" (2 Cor 4:4, italics mine). And in another place he wrote, "I am afraid that just as Eve was deceived by the serpent's cunning, *your minds may somehow be led astray* from your sincere and pure devotion to Christ" (2 Cor 11:3, italics mine).

How can you guard your thoughts? How do you go about putting on the helmet of salvation? I have several suggestions:

First, as Paul writes in 2 Corinthians 10, *you need to make every thought captive to the law of Christ*—put everything you think under his Lordship. This is why we can't live "by bread alone, but... by every word that comes out of God's mouth" (Mt 4:4).

As David observes, "Blessed is the person who meditates day and night on the Word of the Lord" (see Ps 1). The Word of God keeps our thinking moving in the right direction, and protects us from the kind of thinking that is harmful to ourselves and others.

Second, as much as it's possible, *you need to think about good things:* "Whatever is true, whatever is noble, whatever is admirable—if anything is excellent or praiseworthy—*think about these things*" (Phil 4:8, italics mine). "Above all else," Solomon wrote in the Old Testament, "guard your heart, for it is the wellspring of life" (Prv 4:23).

Third, *be careful what you take in with your eyes and ears.* Guard your mind. "Let us throw off everything that hinders and the sin that so easily entangles…. Let us fix our eyes on Jesus" (Heb 12:1-2).

Fourth, *don't trust all your thoughts.* Jeremiah wrote, "The heart is deceitful above all things and beyond cure. Who can understand it?" (Jer 17:9). If you just listen to yourself and have a hard time listening to others, you are setting yourself up for spiritual delusion. An open mind to the counsel and advice of others is a closed door to the mental seduction of dark angels.

FINAL THOUGHTS ON ANGELS

In summary, then, angels dark and light are all around us, influencing circumstances and relationships—and even our thoughts. We need to be aware and wary. "The angel of the Lord camps around those who fear him." We welcome the protection and ministry of good angels when we fear God and keep his commandments. We invite the intrusion of dark angels when we don't. The armor of God is a key to understanding our areas of personal vulnerability, how the Adversary exploits them, and how the Spirit strengthens us to resist him.

Whether or not you believe it, whether or not you know it, angels dark and light are all around you. And what you do, for good or evil, welcomes their participation in your life.

Be self-controlled and vigilant always, for your enemy the devil is always about, prowling like a lion roaring for its prey. Resist him, standing firm in your faith, and remember that the strain is the same for all your fellow Christians in other parts of the world. And after you have borne these sufferings a very little while, the God of all grace, who has called you to share his eternal splendor through Christ, will himself make you whole and secure and strong. All power is his for ever and ever, amen!   1 Peter 5:8-11, PHILLIPS

Appendix 1

Survey Results

In conjunction with a 1993 Doctor of Ministry project for Western Seminary, Phoenix, I did an "angel survey" of several hundred people in three contexts: (1) the adult Bible classes of an independent, charismatic congregation, Word of Grace, where I serve as Senior Minister; (2) two traditional Catholic ministries, including a large, local parish choir and a women's guild; and (3) the adult classes of a large independent, non-charismatic Bible church. In order to insure a minimum level of random sampling, my survey in each of these contexts was limited to those in attendance in the class or club the day the survey was given. The survey itself was not formally tested for reliability and validity.

THE SURVEY

1. Male _____ Female _____
2. Age _____
3. Occupation _____
4. Years of education beyond high school _____
5. Do you believe in the existence of angels?
    Yes _____ No _____
6. Do you know anyone **personally, other than yourself,** who has had an encounter with an angel or angels (an encounter **of any kind**–visual or non-visual, a real angel or an angel in another form, or in a dream)?
    Yes _____ No _____

    If yes, would it be possible for you to share with me their address and/or phone number, so that I could contact them?

7. a. Have you **personally** ever had an encounter with an angel or angels (an encounter **of any kind**–visual or not visual, a real angel or an angel appearing in another form, or in a dream)?

Yes _____ No _____

b. Have you had more than one encounter with an angel/ angels?

Yes _____ No _____

If your answer to the last question, #7, is "no," you're done! If your answer is "yes," please answer the questions in Section 2.

SECTION 2: PART ONE

If you think you have had an angelic encounter, please answer the following questions. Be brief. Please print. Use extra paper if necessary. **If you have had more than one experience,** use extra paper to answer each question separately about each experience. Or you may simply describe the most significant experience.

1. How would you classify your experience? Check only one: You saw an angel...

    ___ With no doubt. You are certain of your experience.

    ___ With some doubt. You had a definite experience, but it was shadowy and you are not entirely sure about what happened.

    ___ With a great deal of doubt, although deep inside you know that something unusual or supernatural occurred.

2. How old were you when the experience occurred?

3. Was/were the angel(s) visible? If so, in what way?

4. How many angels did you see (if more than one)?

5. What was the appearance of the angel(s)? Size, shape, color.

6. Were others present with you when the encounter occurred?
Yes _____ No _____

   If so, did they have a similar experience?
Yes _____ No _____

   Could they confirm what you saw?
Yes _____ No _____

7. Did the angel(s) speak to you? If so, can you remember any portion of the conversation?

SECTION 2: PART TWO

1. Was the experience positive or negative, and in what way?

2. What were the circumstances of your encounter? Were you in a personal crisis, in personal danger, near death, at a crossroads in your life, or did the experience come "out of nowhere"?

3. Did the experience change you life in some way? Are you different today because of the experience? If so, how?

4. Is there anything else you would like to say?

If you have described your encounter with an angel, and would be interested in having your story published, please be sure to include your name, address, and telephone number with your response to this survey. **Optional.**

SURVEY RESULTS

General observations. The results which follow represent my best attempt to assess, synthesize, and categorize an enormous amount of diverse information. The survey was designed to collect specific information, while giving the respondents as much freedom as possible in describing their angel experiences. Consequently, some respondents gave ambiguous or incomplete information, or reported more than one encounter. This explains why some of the column totals may not agree.

I should also point out that some of the responses seemed more credible than others, although the number of improbable stories was relatively small. For the sake of this study, however, I did not make judgments about which stories seemed plausible and which did not. I have given all the respondents the benefit of the doubt by taking their responses at face value and including their responses in my final results.

One factor that in my opinion enhances the credibility of the responses is that with few exceptions people who reported angel encounters had only one or two in their lifetime. In nearly every case, the respondent was able to give his or her specific age when the event occurred. Very few respondents (only eleven of sixty-two who claim to have seen an angel or angels) report multiple encounters with angels, and of those reporting multiple encounters, eight of eleven reported only two. Furthermore, nearly all the other respondents reporting an angel encounter were able to give their specific age at the time the encounter took place. *Only a small portion of the population have had angel experiences, and of those, nearly all are once-in-a-lifetime events.*

It is also important to note that the respondents represent a wide range of ages, from people in their early twenties to those in their seventies; married, single, divorced; male and female; poorly-educated and well-educated; students, homemakers, laborers, and professionals. The respondents do not, however, represent a sampling of the general population, or even of the general Christian population. All of the surveys were circulated in adult Bible classes, a choir, and a Christian service club. We can assume that sub-groupings of the church, like these, represent a generally higher level of Christian life and commitment.

Finally, in surveys of this nature, results can be cataloged and compared in an endless number of combinations. I have chosen to present the results as follows: (1) a grand summary of information provided by all the respondents; (2) a comparison by religious contexts.

ANGELIC ENCOUNTERS

	Number Surveyed	Believe in Angels	Have Seen Angel(s)	Know a person who has seen Angel(s)
Roman Catholic	76	91%	7% (without any doubt: 3%)	7%
Bible Church (Non-Charismatic)	49	100%	33% (without any doubt: 24%)	45%
Charismatic Church	146	100%	28% (without any doubt: 23%)	47%
All Respondents	271	97%	23% (without any doubt: 17%)	35%

CIRCUMSTANCES OF ANGELIC ENCOUNTERS

	Was the Angel Visible?	Purpose of Angel Visit
Roman Catholic (5 out of 76 respondents had a perceived angel encounter)	Human form: 1 Celestial form: 1 In a dream: 1 Not sure: 2	Guidance: 0 Protection: 0 Comfort/Help: 2 At death: 2 Not sure: 1
Bible Church (non-Charismatic) (16 out of 49 respondents had a perceived angel encounter)	Human form: 6 Celestial form: 3 In a dream: 1 Not sure: 6	Guidance: 1 Protection: 6 Comfort/Help: 3 At death: 1 Not sure: 5
Charismatic Church (41 out of 146 respondents had perceived angel encounters)	Human form: 8 Celestial form: 17 In a dream: 2 Not sure: 14	Guidance: 2 Protection: 6 Comfort/Help: 11 At death: 3 Not sure: 19
All respondents (62 out of 271 respondents had perceived angel encounters)	Human form: 24% Celestial form: 34% In a dream: 6% Not sure: 36%	Guidance: 5% Protection: 21% Comfort/Help: 26% At death: 10% Not sure: 38%

EXCERPTS FROM THE SURVEYS

The angel appeared as a "bright, white light." My experience was "positive. I lived through life threatening surgery." I was "near death."

— accountant

"My husband was near death, with congestive heart failure. I was in deep prayer for my husband when the angel entered the pew and sat where my husband usually sat. He had white, wiry hair. He wore a black suit, white shirt, black tie. His suit had white dust all over it." The angel communicated with me "by eye contact only and mental telepathy. He told me not to worry, that my husband would get well and live. My husband is still alive fourteen years later."

— retired medical secretary

"Yes, I saw them. They talked to me. One is always silent, but very comforting. I've seen him in several dreams, always when I'm very troubled." The first time a saw the other angel "I was dying and he told me not to be afraid. He was dressed in a white, hazy robe. The doctors told me I was going to die after the birth of my twins. My case is documented in medical journals. I was literally waiting to die when I had my encounter with the angel in my hospital room." Did the experience change my life somehow? "Absolutely. I have always had a strong faith, but these experiences had a profound effect on my life. According to a Dallas surgical vascular medicine team, I should not be alive today. Miracles do happen!"

— cosmetics sales associate

What was the appearance of the angel? "I only saw what looked like a reflection of a face in the rear view mirror. It had a glow highlighting facial expressions." The encounter was "positive. The experience brought to mind how real angels are and how they can intervene and help us out."

— engineering technician

"I was asleep in my home. The fire alarm went off at 4 A.M. I got up to check the house, but forgot to turn on the lights. After smelling for smoke and not finding anything, I thought maybe it was one of the neighbor's homes. As I was turning the dead bolt on the front door, I sensed someone or something standing behind me. I turned quickly and right behind me was this huge angel—about eight to nine feet tall with a big body. Like a huge man. Vapor-like white. It sort of vaporized in front of me. I immediately knew it was my guardian angel, and I had a sense of being safe in my home."

— school teacher

"I had been a Christian for about one year. I was seeing victory in many areas of my life—except one besetting sin. I was about to fall into that activity again when I was gently picked up under each arm and escorted away from the area and to my vehicle. I did not see anyone, but I felt a pair of strong hands on each arm."

— electronics technician

The angel appeared as "a bright light with radiant color, with the sound of rushing wind." The angel spoke to me, 'Only believe, my child, only believe.'"

— costumer

"Once when my daughter was two years old, she fell out of a chair. I could feel hands and arms around her, and instead of falling, she floated."

— cosmetics consultant

The angels were "very large, shape of a man, but with wings. Their color was not white, but reminded me of a rosy beige. Hair was shoulder length, curled at the ends. The closest one held a large sword upright in his hand."

— homemaker

"I was ten years old. The angel stood in my bedroom doorway with his arms outstretched and told me that I didn't have anything to worry about because God was with me. I had been going through some difficult personal experiences at home. My parents were fighting constantly, and I was being physically abused by my father, emotionally abused by my mother. The experience changed my life, but not until I was twenty-seven. At that time I gave my life to the Lord. When the angel appeared when I was ten, I wasn't sure what this image was, but now, looking back, I realize it was an angel sent by God to let me know that he will never leave me and is always there."

— security officer

The angels were "dazzling white yet transparent. Though it frightened me, it was a positive experience, because I couldn't deny what I saw, and if spirits are real, then God who is Spirit was also real. So the angel experience caused me to search for God earnestly. The experience made it impossible for me to ignore or deny God, no matter how hard I tried. And I did try."

— homemaker

"The angels were not visible to me, but visible to my father—*who did not believe in the supernatural.* He saw several over a period of several minutes the night before he died."

— small business owner

Appendix 2

Glossary of Hebrew and Greek Terms for Angel

OLD TESTAMENT/HEBREW

1. *malak*, messenger, representative, courier, angel. The term used most frequently to designate angelic beings.

   l'k, assumed root of the following:

   malak, messenger, representative

   melaka, work or business

   malakut, message (only in Haggai 1:13)

   "Messenger" is an inadequate term for the range of tasks carried out by the OT *malak*. These were (1) to carry a message, (2) to perform some other specific commission, and (3) to represent more or less officially the one sending him. There were both human and supernatural *melakim*, the latter including the Angel of the Yahweh.[1]

2. *kerubh* or *cherubim* (anglicized, plural)

   These are the first angels to appear in the Bible (Gn 3), as guardians of Eden. They are also referred to as "throne-bearers" for Yahweh. The phrase *Yahweh yosebh hakkerubhim*, Yahweh seated upon the Cherubim, often a direct reference to the Ark of the Covenant, appears in 1 Samuel 4:4; 2 Samuel 6:2; Isaiah 37:16; Psalms 80:1; 99:1.

3. *saraph* or *seraphim* (anglicized, plural)

   It is thought that this term comes from a root word meaning "fire" or "burning." No commonly accepted exact derivation, however, has yet to be found. Gesenius shared the universal doubt as to the origin of this word but considered it best to relate it to the Arabic *sarupha*, to be noble, in that seraphim are the princes or nobles of the heavenly court.[2] "Used only in Isaiah 6:2, 6, these angelic creatures are surely to be compared with the cherubim of the temple decoration and of Ezekiel's later vision. Indeed, the 'living creatures' of Revelation 4 combine elements of Isaiah 6 and Ezekiel 1.... These angelic beings were brilliant as flaming fire."[3]

4. *'abbir*, found only once in the Bible: Psalm 78:25.

5. *'elohim*, God, false gods, godlike beings. The Septuagint translates this term by *angeloi* in Psalms 8:5; 97:7; 138:1, but this may not be the best translation in each case.

6. *beney ha'elohim*, "the sons of God," most notably in the disputed text of Genesis 6:1ff, where the use of the phrase is unclear. Job 1:6, however, seems quite clearly to be a reference to angels.

7. *Gabri'el*, means "man of God" and appears only in Daniel 8:16 and 9:21.

8. *Mikha'el*, appears ten times in the Old Testament. Actually means "one who is as God," suggesting his very lofty position in the angelic hierarchy and the identification of his power with that of God himself.

9. *melis*, "mediator." See Job 33:23.

10. *mesareth*, "ministers," in Psalm 103:21.

11. *'ir*, "watcher." See Job 4:18.

12. *sabha'*, "host." Perhaps "angels" is the meaning of this term in three passages: 1 Kgs 22:19; Neh 9:6; Ps 148:2.

13. *sir*, "envoy." See Isaiah 63:9.

14. *qadhos*, "holy, sacred, that which is set apart." See Psalm 89:6, 7.

15. *qedoshim*, an ambiguous term meaning "Holy Ones," from the Hebrew *qodesh*, holy. Perhaps this word is used for angels, maybe for "the saints," God's holy people. See Ps 89:5; Dn 4:13; Zec 4:14.

NEW TESTAMENT/GREEK

1. *angelos*, messenger, angel, found 175 times in the NT, used of men only six times. Arndt and Gingrich suggest three usages: (1) angels as messengers; (2) intermediary beings generally with no reference to their relation to God; (3) evil spirits.[4]

2. *archangelos*, archangel, or ruling angel.
   "... is found in the NT only in 1 Thessalonians 4:16 and Jude 9. The concept, however, may also be found in Revelation 8:2, 7f., 10, 12; 9:1, 13; 11:15. The only names given are Gabriel (Lk 1:19) and Michael (Jude 9; Rv 12:7)."[5]

3. *isangelos*, like an angel.
   "This rare word occurs in the NT only in Luke 20:36. In the resurrection we shall be 'like the angels,' knowing neither mortality nor marriage."[6]

4. *daimon*, fallen angel.
   Kittel states that the etymology and original meaning of the term are uncertain,[7] yet Brown indicates that *daimon* "is derived from *daiomai*, divide, apportion." It may be connected with the idea of the god of the dead as the divider of corpses."[8]

In popular Greek belief, "*daimones* are (a) spirits of the departed, (b) shades which appear especially in lonely places at night. They cause all kinds of mischances, are responsible for illness and madness, bear special names, and may be warded off or conjured up by magic."[9]

In Judaism we "find the idea of fallen angels, and Satan's angels are called demons. We also read of evil or unclean spirits.... Only rarely here are demons capricious and hurtful. Their main work is to tempt into witchcraft, idolatry, war, bloodshed, and prying into mysteries. Pagans pray to them when seduced into idolatry. They are in opposition to God and owe their position to a fall which implies sin and guilt.... In general the link with the souls of the dead is broken [in other words, in Judaism of this time, demons were not the disembodied spirits of unjust dead persons]."[10]

"*Demonology is adopted [in Judaism] because there is found in us a will that resists observance of the law; this evil will is ascribed to demonic influence, and a relation to Satan is thereby suggested* [italics mine]."[11] According to Brown, the main goal of demons was to lead people into sin.[12]

Brown affirms that in the New Testament "There is no belief in the spirits of the dead or in ghosts.... The fear of demons disappears because of faith in the triumph of Jesus Christ."[13]

Appendix 3

Topical Index of
Angel References in the Bible

Angel/angels:

of the **abyss**, Satan, Rv 9:11

of the **Lord**, Gn 16:7, 11; 18:1-33; 21:17; 22:11-15; 31:11; 32:22-32; 48:15, 16;
Ex 3:2; 4:24; 13:21; 14:19; 23:20; 32:34; 33:2; Nm 20:16; 22:22; Jos 5:15;
Jgs 2:1; 5:23; 6:11; 13:21; 2 Sm 24:16-17; 2 Kgs 1:3; Is 63:9; Hos 12:4; Zec
3:1-6; 12:8; Mal 3:1; Rv 8:3

    as **Jesus**, Zec 3:1-6

as **answers to prayer**, Nm 20:16

appearance of, Gn 19:2-5; 32:22-32; Jgs 13:3-21; 1 Chr 21:16; Dn 9:21; Heb
1:7; Mt 28:2; Lk 24:34; Jn 20:12; Rv 10:1-7; 15:6; 18:1

archangels, 1 Thes 4:16; Jude 1:9

blessing related to obedience, Jgs 2:1-4

of the **bowls of judgment**, Rv 15:6-8; 16:2-17

bread of (manna), Ps 78:25

celebrate salvation, Lk 15:10

cherubim

    appearance of, Ex 37:9; Ez 1:13, 22; 3:13; 10:1-20; 41:18-25; Rv 4:8; 5:8

    and the **Ark of the Covenant**, Ex 25:18-22; 37:7, 9; Nm 7:89; 1 Sm 4:4; 2 Sm
    6:2; 2 Kgs 19:15; 1 Chr 13:6; 28:18; 2 Chr 3:7-14; 5:7-8; Ps 18:10; 80:1;
    99:1; Is 37:16; Heb 9:5

    and the **glory of God, the shekinah**, 2 Sm 22:11; Ez 10:1-20; 11:22; Rv 4:8;
    5:6; 14:3

    as **guardians**, Gn 3:24

    as **heralds**, Rv 6:1, 6

    as **intermediaries**, Rv 5:8

    and **judgment**, Rv 15:7

    as **living creatures**, Ez 1:13-22; 10:15, 20

    as **tabernacle ornamentation**, Ex 26:1, 31; 36:8, 35

    as **temple ornamentation**, 1 Kgs 6:23-35; 7:29,36; 8:6, 7

    as **possible UFOs**, Ez 1:13-22; 3:13; 10:1-20; 11:22

    and **worship**, Rv 4:8,9; 5:11,14; 19:4

and **children**, Mt 18:10

created beings, not divine, Heb 1:5

and **death**, Lk 16:22

deliverance by, Nm 20:16; Is 63:9; Dn 3:28; Acts 5:19; 12:7-15

and **dreams**, Gn 28:12; 31:10-11; Dn 4:13; Mt 1:20, 24; 2:13, 19

show **emotions**, Lk 15:10

encounters should be judged, Gal 1:8

as **entourage of God around the throne,** 1 Kgs 22:19; Neh 9:6; Ps 89:6-8; Rv 3:5; 5:11; 14:10 (see also **glory of God**)

evil, fallen, Mt 25:41; 2 Pt 2:4; 2 Cor 12:7

Gabriel, Dn 8:16; 9:21; Lk 1:19, 26

genderless, Mt 22:30; Mk 12:25

as signs of the **glory of God, the shekinah,** Gn 28:12; Jn 1:51 (see also **cherubim, and Ark of Covenant** and **entourage of God**)

signs of **God's favor,** Gn 32:1

guardian, protection, Gn 48:15-16; Ex 14:19; 23:20-30; 32:34; Ps 34:7; Ps 91:11; Dn 6:22; 12:1; Zec 12:8; Mt 2:13; 4:6; 18:10; 26:53; Lk 4:10; Acts 12:15; Heb 1:13-14; 12:22

as **national guardians,** Dn 12:1

guidance of, Gn 16:9; 21:17; 31:10-11; Ex 3:1-4:17; Nm 22:35; Jgs 6:11-22; 1 Kgs 19:5, 7; 2 Kgs 1:3; Mt 1:20, 24; 2:13, 19; Acts 8:26; 10:3, 4, 7,22; 11:13

as **heralds,** Rv 5:2

as **holy ones,** Dt 33:2, 3; Jb 5:1; 15:15; Ps 89:5, 7; Is 13:3; Dn 4:17; Zec 14:5; 1 Thes 3:13; Jude 14

immortal, Lk 20:36

as **intermediaries,** Rv 8:3

and **Jesus,** Mt 26:53; Mk 1:13; Lk 22:43; Jn 1:51

Jesus greater than, Heb 1:1-14; 2:5-9; 1 Pt 3:22

judged by the saints, 1 Cor 6:3

of **judgment, destroying,** Ex 23:20-30; 32:2; Nm 22:22-35; Jgs 5:23; 2 Sm 24:16-17; 2 Kgs 19:35; 1 Chr 21:12-30; 2 Ps 35:5-6; 78:49; Is 13:3; 37:36; Acts 12:23; 1 Cor 10:10; Rv 7:1-3; 8:5-10:9; 14:15, 19; 15:6; 16:2-17; 17:1; 18:21; 20:1; 22:1, 6

languages of, 1 Cor 13:1

and the **law, the Ten Commandments, Sinai,** Dt 33:2 (implied); Acts 7:38, 53; Gal 3:19; Heb 2:2

life-saving intervention of, Gn 21:17; 32:22-32; 1 Kgs 19:5,7; Jb 33:23; Hos 12:4

living creatures, seraphim, Rv 5:11; 7:11; 15:7 (see also **cherubim**)

witnesses, spectators, observers, Lk 16:22; 1 Cor 4:9; 11:10; 1 Tm 3:16; 5:21; Rv 3:5; 14:10

and **women**, 1 Cor 11:10

as **worshippers of God**, Dt 33:3; Ps 89:5; 103:20; 148:2; Lk 2:13; Heb 1:6; Rv 5:11ff; 7:11

not to be **worshipped**, Rv 22:8-9

Notes

ONE
Frosted Glass: The Enigma of Reality

1. Frederick Buechner, *Wishful Thinking: A Theological ABC* (New York: Harper & Row, 1973), 1-2.

2. C. Fred Dickason, *Angels: Elect and Evil* (Chicago: Moody Press, 1975), 18-19.

3. Karl Barth, *Church Dogmatics: The Doctrine of Creation,* vol. 3, part 3 (Edinburgh: T. & T. Clark, 1961), 410.

4. David Miller, "Angels, Ghosts, and Dreams: The Dreams of Religion and the Religion of Dreams," *The Journal of Pastoral Counseling* 26(1) (1991): 21.

5. As quoted by Mortimer F. Adler, *The Angels and Us* (New York: Macmillan, 1982), 26.

6. Barth, 410-11.

7. Luke 20:35-36, italics mine. This verse contains the only occurrence in the New Testament of the Greek term *isangelos,* "like an angel."

8. The whole account is in Genesis 3:1-7.

9. As quoted in Billy Graham, *Angels: God's Secret Agents* (Garden City, N.Y.: Doubleday, 1975), 17.

10. Timothy Jones, "Rumors of Angels," *Christianity Today* 37(4) (1993): 18-22.

11. I was told this by Paul Pillai, a graduate of Talbot Theological Seminary and a prominent Christian leader in Northern India.

12. Christian scholar Mary Ann Lind writes that "the term *New Age* is a reference to a particular time in the near future when mankind will presumably enter into an era of spiritual enlightenment characterized by the collective realization of the 'god-consciousness' within each person. The universal release of such spiritual power will then usher in a 'new age'" (*From Nirvana to the New Age,* Tarrytown, NY: Revell, 1991, 18). According to Lind, the New Age Movement has also been referred to as the Human Potential Movement, the Aquarian Conspiracy, the Age of Aquarius, the Third Force, and the New Spirituality. Doug Groothuis, perhaps the foremost authority on the New Age, identifies six key elements of the movement: (1) All is one, or monism. Everything—God, human and other forms of life, material and non-material things—in the universe is part of a grand whole. The Karma of Hinduism and "The Force" of *Star Wars* films are expressions of this idea. (2) All is God. God is in everything and God is everything. This is pantheism, where all things are said to partake of the one divine essence. (3) Humanity is God. We are not only perfect; we are in fact, gods. (4) A change in consciousness. Groothuis writes, "All is one; all is god; we are god. Simple enough?" Then why don't we know that? We need to be enlightened. We need to be led into an awareness of oneness and spiritual power. This, incidentally, is precisely what the New Age angels are telling us.

(5) All religious are one. This is, in a word, syncretism. (6) Cosmic evolutionary optimism. A new age is going to dawn, "rising out of the ashes of the Western world view." (See *Unmasking the New Age,* Downers Grove, IL: Intervarsity, 1986, 18-31.)

13. "Dreams are often associated with angels in the Jewish and Christian tradition, as if dreams are themselves in some sense 'angels.'.... The connection of angel and image (dream-image) is common in antiquity. For Philo, in his work *On Giants,* the image of God is the angel or logos. Josephus calls angels *phantasma* ("fantasy images"). In ancient Syriac the word *ekoni* means both image and angel." Miller, 18-28.

14. See 2 Corinthians 12:1-4.

15. Sophy Burnham, *A Book of Angels* (New York: Ballantine Books, 1990), 18.

16. Dickason, *Angels: Elect and Evil,* 23.

TWO
God's Last Word on Angels

1. Job 38:4-7, italics mine. This "poem" is an example of a Hebrew parallelism, which suggests that the parallel ideas in each of the repetitious statements are mutually inclusive. Stars and angels are also implied in Psalm 103:20-21; 148:2-5; and Revelation 1:20.

2. Colin Brown, *The Theological Wordbook of the Old Testament, Three Volumes* (Grand Rapids, Mich.: Zondervan, 1981), vol. 1, 101-2, indicates that popular belief in angels increased in later Judaism. "Angels," he writes, "represented Yahweh's omniscience and omnipresence, formed his court and attendants, and were his messengers. *They were linked with the stars,* the elements, natural phenomena and powers, which they ruled as God's representatives" (italics mine).

3. The meaning of this text is hotly debated. Actually, this is the only place in the Bible where the name "Lucifer" appears, and only in the KJV. Nowhere in the Bible is the name Lucifer specifically assigned to Satan. Satan is called "the Serpent," "the devil," "the dragon," "the destroyer," but not "Lucifer." Yet many students of the Bible, myself included, based on similarities in Ezekiel 28:11-19, Luke 10:18, Revelation 9:1-6, and 12:7-9, believe that this passage is an indirect reference to Satan and his fall from heaven.

4. Here is another verse which suggests a relationship between angels and the stars.

5. Brown, vol. 1, 102.

6. Rob van der Hart, *The Theology of Angels and Devils* (Notre Dame, Ind.: Fides Publishers, 1972), 23.

7. Graham, 18.

8. Collin Brown, vol. 1, 101.

9. Brown, vol. 1, 102.

10. van der Hart, 23.

11. *Sermon on Psalm 103.*

12. Forrester Church, *Entertaining Angels: A Guide to Heaven for Atheists and True Believers* (San Francisco: Harper & Row, 1987), 35.

13. Which means, roughly, "theater (or realm) of devils."

14. Gustav Davidson, *A Dictionary of Angels* (New York: The Free Press, 1969), xiii-xiv.

15. Adler, 45.

16. Graham, 49.

17. Dickason, *Angels: Elect and Evil*, 87.

18. Philip Schaff and Henry Wace, eds., *A Select Library of Nicene and Post-Nicene Fathers of the Christian Church*, Series 1 (Grand Rapids, Mich.: Eerdmans), vol. 3, 256.

19. The word translated "angels" in the KJV and "heavenly beings" in the NIV is the Hebrew word for God, *elohim*. It is evident from the context, and from many other Scriptures, that this word could not be properly translated "God" in this verse.

THREE
Angels Face to Face

1. "Reborn" in the sense of healed inside, not "born again," as in becoming a Christian.

2. Most people have not had an angel encounter of the fourth kind, a face-to-face meeting with a heavenly being. And those who have, have met an angel only once or twice in a lifetime.

3. Survey content and results are detailed in Appendix 1.

4. Although the gender of angels is not specifically identified in the Bible, it is worth noting that in the Greek text of the New Testament, "angel" is always found in the masculine form, never feminine or neuter.

5. Graham, 23.

6. We will investigate the use of the phrase "the angel of the Lord" in chapter 8.

7. Some people are into reading "personal auras," the kinds and colors of light that supposedly represent our personalities. This practice is strictly cultic.

8. Joan Webster Anderson, *Where Angels Walk: True Stories of Heavenly Visions* (Sea Cliff, N.Y.: Barton and Brett, 1992), 22.

9. Theodora Ward, *Men and Angels* (New York: Viking Press, 1969), 7, italics mine.

10. See Ezekiel 10:20.

11. Davidson.

FOUR
What Good Angels Do for a Living

1. Barth, 479.

2. Adler, 69.

3. Ephesians 1:18ff and 3:10.

4. This is not a good model for relating to people with differing religious views! Our understanding of how to relate to our enemies has been reshaped by the teaching of Jesus and the New Testament.

5. As quoted in *Angels Among Us* (Carmel, N.Y.: Guideposts Associates, 1993), 62.

6. As quoted in Jean Danielou, *The Angels and Their Mission: According to the Fathers of the Church* (Westminster, Md.: Christian Classics, Inc., 1976), 75.

7. John Calvin, *Calvin's Institutes* (Grand Rapids, Mich.: Associated Publishers, n.d.), 77.

8. Gary D. Kinnaman, *Overcoming the Dominion of Darkness* (Old Tappan, N.J.: Fleming Revell/Chosen, 1990, 54.

9. Dickason, *Angels, Elect and Evil,* 92.

10. Philip Schaff, ed., *A Select Library of the Nicene and Post-Nicene Fathers of the Christian Church,* Series 2, (Grand Rapids, Mich.: Eerdmans, 1983), vol.2, 162.

11. Basilea Schlink, *The Unseen World of Angels and Demons* (Old Tappan, N.J.: Fleming Revell, 1985), 81.

12. Dickason, *Angels, Elect and Evil,* 92.

13. Acts 12:21-23. This account was undoubtedly intended by Luke to be a warning to Roman leaders. When Acts was written, the Roman emperor, Caesar, considered himself to be God, or at least a god. Additionally, he expected the people of the Roman empire to acknowledge him as God. Luke's message is that God will not tolerate that kind of thinking, and to see oneself as divine, or near to it, is to invite a visit from the angel of death.

14. A. Cleveland Coxe, ed., *The Ante-Nicene Fathers: Translations of the Writings of the Fathers down to A.D. 325* (Grand Rapids, Mich.: Eerdmans, 1951), vol. 4, 544.

15. Burnham, 20. I want to remind the reader that Burnham's book, which has sold over one-half million copies, is decidedly New Age. Portions of her book, however, are quite informative.

FIVE
Your Personal Angel

1. Brown, vol. 1, 101-2.

2. Schaff and Wace, Series 1, vol. 13, 272. Chrysostom is basing his teaching on a loose translation of Genesis 48:15, 16.

3. Coxe, vol. 8, 48. This was written circa 240 A.D.

4. As quoted in Danielou, 69.

5. As quoted in Danielou, 68.

6. As quoted in Pascal P. Parente, *Beyond Space: A Book about Angels* (Rockford, Ill.: Tan Books and Publishers, 1973), 126. I have paraphrased the quotation slightly to simplify the old English.

7. As quoted in Danielou, 70, italics mine.

8. Danielou, 68-69, italics mine.

9. Burnham, 136.

10. As quoted in Danielou, 81.

11. Danielou, 71.

12. The fourteen apocryphal books were always considered sacred literature in the general sense, but they were not a part of the canon of Holy Scripture until five hundred years ago. These books were recognized as "deutero-canonical" by the Catholic Church at the Council of Trent. These books are not included in Protestant Bibles, however, as Protestants do not consider them to have the same authority as Scripture.

13. Parente, 126.

14. Origen, as quoted in Danielou, 80.

15. As quoted and discussed in Adler, 73.

16. See Appendix 3, a comprehensive index of Scripture references on angels.

17. This story is used by permission of Fleming H. Revell. Corrie ten Boom with Elizabeth Sherrill *The Hiding Place* (Grand Rapids, Mich.: Fleming H./ Revell,. 1984).

18. As quoted in *Angels Among Us,* 56.

SIX
Angels on the Edge of Death

1. Graham, 152.

2. Luke 16:19ff., especially verse 22.

3. Moses appeared with Elijah on the Mount of Transfiguration, perhaps anticipating the reappearance of both Elijah and Moses prior to the Last Day, as suggested in Revelation 11.

4. Parente, 129.

5. George Gallup, *Adventures in Immortality: A Look Beyond the Threshold of Death* (New York: McGraw-Hill, 1982), 91-92.

6. Raymond A. Moody, Jr., *Life after Life: Actual Case Histories that Reveal There Is Life after Death* (New York: Bantam Books, 1975), 21.

7. Naomi Cutner, *et al.* "At the Edge of Eternity," *Life* (March 1992), 71.

8. Cutner, 71.

9. Cutner, 68.

SEVEN
Angels in Disguise

1. *Angels Among Us,* 11.

EIGHT
Archangels, Beasts, and UFOs

1. From the *Talmud,* as cited by A.C. Gaebelein, *What the Bible Says about Angels* (Grand Rapids, Mich.: Baker Book House, 1987), 20.

2. Calvin, 76, italics mine.

3. For a complete list of the references to Michael, see the topical index of angel texts in Appendix 3.

4. Gesenius, as cited by William George Heidt, *Angelology of the Old Testament: A Study in Biblical Theology* (Washington, D.C.: Catholic University of America Press, 1949), 15.

5. Robert H. Mounce, *The New International Commentary on the New Testament: The Book of Revelation* (Grand Rapids, Mich.: Eerdmans, 1977), 135-36. See also 1 Chronicles 24:4; 25:9-13.

6. See especially Revelation 11:14.

7. An exhaustive list of Hebrew and Greek angel terms can be found in Appendix 2.

8. Genesis 6:1-2, 4, italics mine. For a thorough exegesis of this passage see Victor P. Hamilton, *The New International Commentary on the Old Testament: The Book of Genesis,* chapters 1-17 (Grand Rapids, Mich.: Eerdmans, 1990), 261-72. He concludes, "Suffice it to say, it is impossible to be dogmatic about the identification of 'sons of God' here. The best one can do is to consider the options. While it may not be comforting to the reader, perhaps it is best to say that the evidence is ambiguous and therefore defies clear-cut identifications and solutions" (p. 265).

9. See Daniel 9:21. William Hendriksen, *More Than Conquerors: An Interpretation of the Book of Revelation* (Grand Rapids, Mich.: Baker Book House, 1970), 107.

10. Graham, 14.

11. Graham, 11.

12. Most of what follows in this section on UFOs is drawn from Mark Albrecht and Brooks Alexander, "UFOs: Is Science Fiction Coming True?" *Spiritual Counterfeits Journal* (August 1977), 12-23. Albrecht and Alexander in turn acknowledge that a large part of their research was based on John Weldon's *UFOs: What on Earth Is Happening?*, originally published by Harvest House and reprinted by Bantam Books.

13. In their article on UFOs, Albrecht and Alexander discuss the "mechanics of spiritual power." John Keel is further quoted, "The statistical data... indicate that flying saucers are *not* stable machines.... They are, in all probability, transmogrifications of energy and do not exist in the same way that this book exists. They are not permanent constructions of matter." Dr. Curt Wagner, a physicist with a Ph.D. in general relativity theory, agreed with Keel's assessment. In an interview with Spiritual Counterfeits Project staff, Dr. Wagner said, "Drawing from what we know can happen in seances and poltergeist activity, it seems that these supernatural forces can manipulate matter and energy, extracting energy from the atmosphere, for example (which manifests as a local temperature

change), to manipulate matter and produce an apparent violation of the second law [of thermodynamics], and I guess my feeling is that on a larger scale that is what a UFO could be. I'm not saying that I know that it is, but only that it could be. It seems to me likely that UFOs are large-scale violations of the second law in which energy is arranged so that it appears to look like matter, yet it's really just an energy concentration—it's not really solid matter in the usual sense."

14. Scott, as quoted in Albrecht and Alexander, described them as "ugly, with sloping shoulders, crocodile-scaled skin, elephant-like feet, and hands with three fingers and a recessed thumb."

NINE
Hell's Angels

1. Horst Balz and Gerhard Schneider, eds., *Exegetical Dictionary of the New Testament* (Grand Rapids, Mich.: Eerdmans, 1993), vol. 2, 234.

2. Matthew 9:34; 12:24. The meaning of Beelzebub is uncertain. Brown (vol. 3, 469) suggests that "most probably *Bee(l)zeboul* comes from *ba'al zibbul* (from post Old Testament Hebrew. *Zebel* manure, dung; *zibbul* meaning an idolatrous sacrifice)—lord of the idol-sacrifice—which is at once equalled to dung."

3. Dickason, *Angels, Elect and Evil,* 141ff.

4. Dickason, *Angels, Elect and Evil,* 155. The general discussion which follows is based on Dickason's chapter "The Derivation of Demons," 155-60.

5. Angels are "spirits" in Hebrews 1:14, while demons are termed "spirits" in Matthew 8:16.

6. Coxe, vol. 1, 190.

7. John Warwick Montgomery, *Principalities and Powers: A Fascinating Look at the Paranormal, the Supernatural, and the Hidden Things* (Minneapolis: Bethany House, 1973), 142.

8. Burnham, 128.

9. In 1 Peter 3:18-20, an obscure and perplexing Scripture, the apostle tells us that Jesus, between the time he died on the cross on Friday and rose from the dead on Sunday, "went and preached to the spirits in prison [that is, hades], who disobeyed long ago when God waited patiently in the days of Noah while the ark was being built." Peter doesn't tell us why Jesus limited his preaching to spirits from the time of Noah. Nor does he tell us what Jesus said when he preached to them, or even why he preached to them at all. Or what happened at the end of his sermon. It's also not clear if these "spirits" were people or angels. Some think that this explains why some of the angels are bound in the pit, that is, the fallen angels who were directly responsible for the wickedness at the time of the Flood. I think, rather, that they were people, because there is nothing else anywhere in the Bible to suggest that a certain company of angels fell into sheol at the time of the Flood.

TEN

What Dark Angels Do for a Living

1. Hal Mattern, "Believe in Ghosts?" *The Arizona Republic,* Oct. 31, 1991, 1.

2. Mickey Hart, *Drumming at the Edge of Magic: A Journey into the Spirit of Percussion* (New York: HarperCollins, 1990), 15.

3. Hart, 180.

4. Hart, 181.

5. Albrecht and Alexander, 20.

6. The person who shared this experience with me is a fairly new Christian who is attending our church regularly. For obvious reasons, I have decided in this case to allow the person to remain anonymous.

7. Matthew and Dennis Linn, *Deliverance Prayer* (New York: Paulist Press, 1981), 5, 7.

8. C. Fred Dickason, *Demon Possession and the Christian: A New Perspective* (Westchester, Ill.: Crossway Books, 1987), 40.

9. As cited by Charles Kraft, *Defeating Dark Angels: Breaking Demonic Oppression in the Believer's Life* (Ann Arbor, Mich.: Vine Books, 1992), 37-38.

10. Kraft, 37.

11. Jesse Penn-Lewis, *War on the Saints* (Fort Washington, Pa.: Christian Literature Crusade, 1977; original edition, 1912), 69.

12. I recommend *Defeating Dark Angels,* by Charles Kraft (Vine Books, 1992); *Demon Possession and the Christian,* by C. Fred Dickason (Crossway Books, 1987); and *Exorcism: Fact or Fiction,* by Ken Olson (Thomas Nelson, 1992).

13. Michael Scanlan and Randall Cirner, *Deliverance from Evil Spirits: A Weapon for Spiritual Warfare* (Ann Arbor, Mich.: Servant Books, 1980), 63ff.

14. Linn and Linn, 7.

15. Kinnaman, 177-78.

16. Front cover of the *Atlantic Monthly,* April, 1993.

17. Kraft, 74.

18. David Peterson, *Engaging with God: A Biblical Theology of Worship* (Grand Rapids, Mich.: Eerdmans, 1992), 24-25.

19. Calvin, 77.

20. As quoted in Kinnaman, 54-55.

21. Clinton E. Arnold, *Powers of Darkness: Principalities and Powers in Paul's Letters* (Downer's Grove, Ill.: InterVarsity Press, 1992), 98.

22. Arnold, 99.

23. Arnold, 100.

ELEVEN

A New Age of Angels

1. Alma Daniel, Timothy Wyllie, and Andrew Ramer, *Ask Your Angels: A Practical Guide to Working with the Messengers of Heaven to Empower and Enrich Your*

Life (New York: Ballantine Books, 1992), 39-40.

2. Daniel, *et al.*, 26-27.

3. John Naisbitt and Patricia Aburdene, *Megatrends 2000: Ten New Directions for the 1990s* (New York: William Morrow, 1990), 271.

4. *National and International Religion Report*, September 6, 1993, 7.

5. Randolf Price, *The Angels Within Us: A Spiritual Guide to the Twenty-two Angels that Govern Our Lives* (New York: Fawcett/Columbine/Ballantine, 1993), 2-3.

6. Price, 7.

7. Daniel, *et al.*, 27-29, italics mine.

8. John Stott, "Joseph Smith's 1823 Vision: Uncovering the Angel Message," *Religion*, vol. 18, 1988, 348. See also Dean C. Jessee, *The Personal Writings of Joseph Smith* (Salt Lake City: Deseret Book Company, 1984), 6-7.

9. Oscar W. McConkie, *Angels* (Salt Lake City: Deseret Book Company, 1975), 27, italics mine.

10. This is not the Aaronic priesthood of the Old Testament. The Aaronic Priesthood for Mormons is a specially appointed and ordained counsel of spiritual leaders who receive ongoing guidance from angels.

11. McConkie, 86-87.

12. Davidson, xi.

13. Price, 9.

14. Price, 5.

15. J. Rodman Williams, "Angels on Assignment: A Paper from Melodyland School of Theology" (Anaheim, Calif.: Melodyland School of Theology, n.d., unpublished), 7. The quotation is from Roland Buck, as told to Charles and Frances Hunter, *Angels on Assignment* (Houston, Tex.: Hunter Books, 1979), 45.

16. Terry Lynn Taylor, *Guardians of Hope* (Tiburon, Calif.: H.J. Kramer, 1992), 91-93.

17. Williams, 12. Quotation is from Buck, 59.

18. Barth, 372.

TWELVE
In the Line of Fire

1. According to the Church Growth Resource Center, Boliver, Mo.

2. Howard Snyder and Daniel Runyon, *Foresight: Ten Major Trends that Will Dramatically Affect the Future of Christians and the Church* (Nashville: Thomas Nelson, 1986), 68.

3. As quoted in Snyder and Runyon, 69.

4. As quoted in Snyder and Runyon, 69.

5. Ron Boehme, *Leadership for the 21st Century: Changing Nations Through the Power of Serving* (Seattle: YWAM Publishers/Frontline Communications, 1989), 188, italics mine.

6. As quoted in Boehme, 44.

7. The KJV uses the expression "have dominion." There has been no little debate in recent years over "dominion theology." The kingdom of God, as I understand it, is eternal and spiritual, but with profound implications for time and

earth. What happens in the heavenlies, as we have shown throughout this book, influences what happens in this life, here and now. I do not hold the position, however, that the advance of the kingdom means that somehow the church will "christianize" the world's systems. The sword will become a plow irreversibly only when Christ comes again in glory to judge the living and the dead. Then and only then will the kingdom be fully realized, as the old heaven and earth pass away.

8. As quoted by Donald W. Dayton, *Theological Roots of Pentecostalism* (Grand Rapids, Mich.: Zondervan, 1987), 155.

THIRTEEN
Welcoming the Light, Withstanding the Darkness

1. Geddes MacGregor, *Angels: Ministers of Grace* (New York: Paragon House Publishers, 1987), 199.

2. Gordon Fee notes that "this passage is full of notorious exegetical difficulties" (p. 492). In other words, any attempt to unravel the meaning of 1 Corinthians 11 would be an undertaking well beyond the purpose of this book. I refer the reader to Fee's commentary for further insight: *The New International Commentary on the New Testament: 1 Corinthians* (Grand Rapids, Mich.: Eerdmans, 1987).

3. Fee, 521.

4. Fee, 521.

5. Henry Theissen, *Lectures in Systematic Theology* (Grand Rapids, Mich.: Eerdmans, 1949), 207.

6. As quoted in Danielou, 82.

7. Danielou, 81.

8. *Time,* December 27, 1993.

9. One chapter is on "Group Visualization for Planetary Healing."

10. Daniel, *et al.,* 167.

11. Daniel, *et al.,* 173.

12. W. Robertson Nicoll, ed., *The Expositor's Greek Testament* (Grand Rapids, Mich.: Eerdmans, 1974), vol. 3, 386.

13. M. Scott Peck, *People of the Lie: The Hope for Healing Human Evil* (New York: Simon & Schuster, 1983), 207. Scott Peck is widely read and is noted to be a Christian psychiatrist, although portions of his writings are decidedly unorthodox.

14. Merrill Unger, *Demons in the World Today* (Wheaton, Ill.: Tyndale, 1971), 116.

15. Kinnaman, 127.

Appendix 2

Glossary of Hebrew and Greek Terms for Angel

1. R. Laird Harris, ed., *Theological Word Book of the Old Testament,* 2 vols. (Chicago: Moody, 1980), vol. 1, 464-65.

2. Heidt, 15.

3. Harris, vol. 2, 884.

4. William F. Arndt and Wilbur F. Gingrich, *A Greek-English Lexicon of the New Testament and Other Early Christian Literature* (Chicago: the University of Chicago Press, 1957), 7-8.

5. Brown, vol. 1, 103.

6. Gerhard Kittel and Gerhard Friedrich, eds., *Theological Dictionary of the New Testament* abridged in one volume by Geoffrey Bromily. (Grand Rapids, Mich.: Eerdmans/Paternoster, 1985), 14.

7. Kittel and Friedrich, 137.

8. Brown, vol. 1, 450.

9. Kittel and Friedrich, 138.

10. Kittel and Friedrich, 139.

11. Kittel and Friedrich, 139.

12. Brown, vol. 1, 451.

13. Brown, vol. 1, 452.

Recommended Reading

Adler, Mortimer F. *The Angels and Us.* New York: MacMillan, 1982.

Albrecht, Mark, and Brooks Alexander. "UFOs: Is Science Fiction Coming True?" *Spiritual Counterfeits Journal.* August 1977, 12-23.

Arnold, Clinton E. *Powers of Darkness: Principalities and Powers in Paul's Letters.* Downer's Grove, Ill.: InterVarsity Press, 1992.

Barth, Karl. *Church Dogmatics: The Doctrine of Creation,* vol. 3, part 3. Edinburgh: T. & T. Clark, 1961.

Danielou, Jean. *The Angels and Their Mission: According to the Fathers of the Church.* Westminster, Md.: Christian Classics, Inc., 1976.

Dickason, C. Fred. *Angels: Elect and Evil.* Chicago: Moody Press, 1975.

Dickason, C. Fred. *Demon Possession and the Christian: A New Perspective.* Westchester, Ill.: Crossway Books, 1987.

Gaebelein, A. C. *What the Bible Says about Angels.* Grand Rapids, Mich.: Baker Book House, 1987.

Graham, Billy. *Angels: God's Secret Agents.* Garden City, N.Y.: Doubleday, 1975.

Jones, Timothy. "Rumors of Angels." *Christianity Today* 37(4) (1993): 18-22.

Kinnaman, Gary D. *Overcoming the Dominion of Darkness.* Old Tappan, N.J.: Fleming Revell/Chosen, 1990.

Kraft, Charles. *Defeating Dark Angels: Breaking Demonic Oppression in the Believer's Life.* Ann Arbor, Mich.: Vine Books, 1992.

Lewis, C.S. *The Screwtape Letters.* New York: MacMillan, 1962.

Linn, Matthew, and Dennis Linn. *Deliverance Prayer.* New York: Paulist Press, 1981.

Montgomery, John Warwick. *Principalities and Powers: A Fascinating Look at the Paranormal, the Supernatural, and the Hidden Things.* Minneapolis: Bethany House, 1973.

Morse, Melvin. *Closer to the Light: Learning From the Near-Death Experiences of Children.* New York: Ivy Books, 1990.

Olsen, Ken. *Exorcism: Fact or Fiction.* Nashville: Thomas Nelson, 1992.

Penn-Lewis, Jesse. *War on the Saints.* Fort Washington, Pa.: Christian Literature Crusade, 1977 (original edition, 1912).

Scanlan, Michael, and Randall Cirner. *Deliverance from Evil Spirits: A Weapon for Spiritual Warfare.* Ann Arbor, Mich.: Servant Books, 1980.

Schlink, Basilea. *The Unseen World of Angels and Demons.* Old Tappan, N.J.: Fleming Revell, 1985.

Swilhart, Stephen D. *Angels in Heaven and Earth.* Plainfield, N.J.: Logos, 1979.

Index of Names and Subjects